Greek accents are a seen
of the New Testament.

through the fog in a pedagogically humane way. Well laid out and easy to digest, this book offers a straightforward, step-by-step approach to the acquisition of Greek accentuation for any who want to master this language. I recommend it even for the beginner because knowledge of the accents is essential for learning the language properly from the get-go. It is much easier to have good habits of pronunciation from the start than to unlearn bad habits later on.

Daniel B. Wallace, senior research professor,
New Testament, Dallas Theological Seminary

With admiral clarity and simplicity John Lee introduces the rules of Greek accentuation in eight short lessons. Accents are rarely taught, though central to advanced Greek study; and no other resource makes learning accents easier and explains their complexities in a more accessible fashion. Every serious student should study this book.

James K. Aitken, reader in Hebrew and
early Jewish studies, University of Cambridge

There is simply no better place to start learning Greek accentuation than right here with this book.

Constantine R. Campbell, professor of New
Testament, Trinity Evangelical Divinity School

A really useful little book!

Eleanor Dickey, FBA, professor of classics,
University of Reading, England

In G. K. Chesterton's autobiography he writes, "As for Greek accents, I triumphantly succeeded, through a long series of school-terms, in avoiding learning them at all." If many a Greek teacher is honest, his or her knowledge of Greek accents may not be too far behind Chesterton's. Thankfully, in this compact and well-written new book, John Lee guides both professors and students to a competency in Greek accents. Thanks are due to Dr. Lee for producing a resource that has been needed for generations.

> **Robert L. Plummer,** professor of New Testament
> interpretation, The Southern Baptist Theological
> Seminary, founder of Daily Dose of Greek

John A. L. Lee is both a distinguished authority on ancient Greek and an outstanding classroom teacher. This compact book, beautifully produced, dispels the unnecessary mystique that has come to shroud the topic of ancient Greek accents, offering a clear and practical approach to rapid mastery of the basic rules and patterns of usage. The book is best suited to use in the classroom context, but it can also be used effectively for private study. It functions as a highly accessible guide for those taking their first steps in Greek accentuation, while experts too will find valuable insights here. I strongly recommend it to all teachers of the language.

> **T. V. Evans,** associate professor, ancient languages
> program director, Macquarie University

From the author of the magisterial *History of New Testament Lexicography*, here comes an eminently useful and practical tool on Greek accents—for students, teachers, and editors alike. Highly recommended.

> **Andreas Köstenberger,** senior research professor of
> New Testament and biblical theology, Southeastern
> Baptist Theological Seminary, and founder of Biblical
> Foundations™ (www.biblicalfoundations.org)

Basics

— *of* —

Greek
Accents

**EIGHT LESSONS
WITH EXERCISES**

John A. L. Lee

ZONDERVAN

Basics of Greek Accents
Copyright © 2018 by John A. L. Lee

This title is also available as a Zondervan ebook.

Requests for information should be addressed to:
Zondervan, *3900 Sparks Dr. SE, Grand Rapids, Michigan 49546*

Library of Congress Cataloging-in-Publication Data

Names: Lee, John A. L., 1942- author.
Title: Basics of Greek accents : eight lessons with exercises / John A.L. Lee.
Description: Grand Rapids, MI : Zondervan, [2018] | Includes bibliographical
    references and index.
Identifiers: LCCN 2017046170 | ISBN 9780310555643 (softcover)
Subjects: LCSH: Greek language—Accents and accentuation. | Greek language,
    Biblical—Accents and accentuation.
Classification: LCC PA269 .L37 2018 | DDC 481/.6—dc23 LC record available at
    https://lccn.loc.gov/2017046170

First published in 2005 by Ancient History Documentary Research Centre, Macquarie
University, Sydney 2109 Australia. Copyright © 2005 John A. L. Lee.

Any Internet addresses (websites, blogs, etc.) and telephone numbers in this book are
offered as a resource. They are not intended in any way to be or imply an endorsement
by Zondervan, nor does Zondervan vouch for the content of these sites and numbers
for the life of this book.

The cover image is of Romans 14:22–23:

Μακάρϊος ὁ μὴ κρίνων ἑαυτὸν
ἐν ᾧ δοκϊμάζει· ὁ δὲ δϊακρϊ
νόμενος, ἐὰν φάγῃ κατακέ
κρϊται. ὅτϊ οὐκ ἐκ πϊστεως

The image is from the Special Collections Library of the University of Michigan, Mich
Ms. 34. Digitized by The Center for the Study of New Testament Manuscripts (www
.csntm.org), GA 223 0144a, parchment codex, XIV AD. Used with permission. See
illustration 3 (pp. 96–99) for full text and notes.

Cover design: Veldheer Creative Services
Cover photo: Special Collections Library / University of Michigan
Interior design: Kait Lamphere

Printed in the United States of America

18 19 20 21 22 23 24 25 26 /DHV/ 15 14 13 12 11 10 9 8 7 6 5 4 3 2 1

Contents

Preface

At a time when Greek accents are increasingly passed over in the classroom, even by teachers of the Classical language, a new tool for learning Greek accentuation may seem pointless. The opposite is true. Accents are an integral part of the Greek writing system inherited from antiquity. Ignoring them in the early stages of learning may seem an easy option, but sooner or later the lack of knowledge will be missed by anyone who continues with Greek. For advanced research and publication their use is indispensible. It may also be thought that there are enough guides already. But the existing handbooks, though good in their way, do not really meet the need, as is explained in the bibliography.

This book began life as a short course for an informal class held at Macquarie University, Sydney, in 2004, and gradually grew from that. I am grateful to the members of that first class for providing the occasion to construct such a course and for the contribution they made by their enthusiasm and their questions. A first edition in A4 format was printed in 2005 under the auspices of the Ancient History Documentary Research Centre (as it then was) at Macquarie University. Alanna

Nobbs's support of that enterprise is gratefully acknowledged. I am happy to record again my thanks to John Sheldon for checking through that edition before publication and offering many helpful comments. Subsequently the course was used with classes a number of times, each providing opportunities for improvement. The review by Trevor Evans in *Classicum* 33.1 (2007): 31 contributed further, and subsequently Trevor discussed several issues with me and helped me resolve them. He has kindly read the revised version in full, a labour I much appreciate.

In this new edition, no major changes to the structure have been needed. Only improvements to the layout and minor additions to the content have been made. Two new sections have been added, "Traditional Accent Terminology" and "Illustrations," intended to provide useful information—and visual pleasure—regarding the history of Greek accents. I am grateful to the publisher, Zondervan, for showing an interest in the work, and especially to Chris Beetham, Senior Editor, for his enthusiastic support from the beginning, his ongoing encouragement, and his important input at copy-editing stage.

JL
October 2017

Introduction

Mortified, I resolved to learn principles of accentuation so well I would never be caught short again.

  —D. A. Carson, *Greek Accents: A Student's Manual*

Make sure of your accents at all times. Nothing so quickly repels a Greek scholar as false accents.

      —Herbert Youtie, in Klaas A. Worp,
            "Youtie's 'Guidelines.'"

True competence in Greek cannot be attained without competence in Greek accents.

           —John Lee

The aim of this book is strictly practical: to teach the basics of Greek accentuation to anyone who has already learnt some Greek but who, for whatever reason, has an unsure grasp of Greek accents or no grasp at all. It does not attempt to cover every detail. The beginner cannot cope with an exhaustive treatment, and there are good reference books that can be consulted once the basics are known. Exercises are included, for use both in class and at home. Building confidence is an important part of what is needed. Theory is not discussed.

The course was created for use by a class and teacher, but it can also be used by a student working alone—provided the essential ingredient, application, is present. Answers to the exercises are supplied. Those who have some knowledge of accents may also find it useful as a refresher course or handy guide to the essentials.

Advice to the teacher. A class of one hour per week over eight weeks is the optimum. The best procedure is for the teacher to take the class through the material of the lesson in the first half hour or so, reading over the rules and examples, and adding explanations where appropriate. A controlled selection of examples has been given: not too much more should be added. Often a form is given as a trigger for the full declension or conjugation, as, for example, χώρα in lesson 3. Here the teacher can ask the class to call to mind the rest of the declension, quickly run through it, and remind students that if they are unsure of the forms they should look them up in their favourite grammar book when writing the accents. The teacher must judge how many to treat in this way; they cannot all be done in the time allotted. *Pronunciation aloud by both teacher and class in the course of the lesson is essential.*

The latter half of the hour should be given to the class exercise: for each lesson there is one designed to be done on the spot by all the class, working individually. (Rather than write in the book, it may be useful to make photocopies of the exercises.) Once the class has begun work, the teacher can walk around, looking at each student's work as it progresses. This gives an opportunity to help where necessary, identify problems, and give encouragement. It can often be useful to call everyone's attention to some point that has arisen. The exercise is a little long for the time, and not all students will finish it, but it presents a useful challenge. Finally, the homework should be set, to be handed in before or at the next class. Needless to say, the course is best run by a teacher who has a confident knowledge of Greek accents. But if this is not possible, there is no reason why teacher and class cannot embark on the journey of learning together.

Advice to the student working alone. It is best to replicate the classroom pattern as much as possible. Set aside some time each week to work through the lesson and do the class exercise. Have your favourite grammar on hand for reference to standard forms. Do *not* look at the answers until after the exercise is done. Then do the homework exercise at a later time, when the material in the lesson has had a chance to sink in. Finally, try at all costs to have a short session with someone who knows the accents well and can check some of your exercises and answer questions. And don't forget to *pronounce the words aloud.*

Pronunciation. We all know that the accentuation originally indicated a pitch accent. But in my opinion the only practical method today is to use a stress accent, as became standard later in the language. That is, a stress is placed on the syllable where the accent is marked. An acute is always stressed, a circumflex mostly, and a grave is usually unstressed but is stressed in certain cases (e.g., in σοφὸς ἀνήρ). Guidance from a teacher is desirable here. Students should be urged to learn any word or inflection with its accent when first encountered, and to maintain that pronunciation at all times. Teachers should lead the way by example.

The course is designed for students of Ancient Greek, whether Classical or Koine. The vocabulary and exercises draw on both. Lesson 8 covers somewhat more advanced material than most students will want or need. The items there are presented in descending order of importance; some can be passed over in class, but they are useful to have for reference.

No one can master Greek accents in eight lessons. In fact, a lifetime hardly suffices. But reasonable competence and confidence can be quickly acquired. Accents are not nearly as hard as they seem, and putting off learning them only makes them harder. There is also satisfaction to be gained from meeting the challenge they offer. They can even be fun.

LESSON 1

The Basic Rules

The basics of Greek accentuation are not complicated. Much depends on observation of the length of vowels. Knowing these is the first step toward becoming confident in the use of accents. Though it would be possible to formulate a "rule" for every detail of how the accents work, the approach in this book is to encourage familiarity with *patterns*. Some rules will be given, but not many. In this lesson there are only four. But first we need some preliminary and essential information.

Vowel length. To place accents correctly, one needs to be aware of the length of any vowel. The vowels are regarded as **long** or **short**, as follows:

Short: ε, ο
Long: η, ω, including ῃ, ῳ, also ᾳ
Short *or* long: α, ι, υ
"Diphthongs" are long: αι, ει, οι, αυ, ευ, ου, υι, ηυ, and
    ωυ, except that final -αι, -οι are short.[1]

---

1. Though note that final -αι, -οι are long in the optative (see lesson 8).

Accent marks. The accent marks are three in number. They are used in different ways, according to the syllable on which they can appear and the length of the vowel.

- Acute (ά) can be on the **last**, **second-last**, or **third-last** syllable, and on a long or short vowel. Examples: θεός, λόγος, ἀπόστολος, προφήτης, θεοί

- Circumflex (ᾶ) can be on the **last** or **second-last** syllable, but only on a *long* vowel. Examples: καλῶς, δοῦλος

- Grave (ὰ) can only be on the **last** syllable, and may be on a long or short vowel. It is used when a final acute changes to a grave, before another word following without any mark of punctuation.[2] Examples: τὸν θεόν. τὸν θεόν, τὸν θεὸν . . ., τὴν τιμὴν . . .

Writing of Accents:

An accent is written on the second vowel of a diphthong: τούς, τοῖς

Accents are combined with breathings like this: ἄ, ἅ, ἦ, οὔ, οὗ, Ἄ, ἇ . . .

The circumflex in tilde form (ᾶ) is sometimes seen.

---

2. If the following word is an enclitic, different rules apply (see lesson 7).

Length of Last Syllable and the Four Rules

The length of the last syllable of a word plays a significant role in determining the position of the accent. This leads to four basic rules of Greek accentuation:

1. If the last syllable is **short**, the accent may be on the *last, second-last*, or *third-last* syllable. Example: ἄνθρωπος
2. If the last syllable is **long**, the accent may be on the *last* or *second-last* syllable, but *not* third-last. Example: ἀνθρώπου
3. If the last syllable is **long and the accent is on the second-last**, the accent must be acute (*not* circumflex). Example: δούλου
4. If the last syllable is **short and the accent is on the second-last which is long**, the accent must be circumflex.[3] Example: δοῦλος

Notice that an accent may appear on any of the last *three* syllables, but not any further from the end of a word.

A Fixed Pattern

In the declension of nouns with an accent on the last syllable (and words like the article), an *acute* in the nominative and

---

3. This is often called the "σωτῆρα rule," as a good example of the pattern.

accusative becomes a *circumflex* in the genitive and dative (both singular and plural). Examples:

θεός, θεόν, θεοῦ, θεῷ   τό, τό, τοῦ, τῷ
θεοί, θεούς, θεῶν, θεοῖς   τά, τά, τῶν, τοῖς

The Golden Rule of Accents

If in doubt, check! (Or: know what you don't know.)

Illustrations

Look through this list and observe how the four basic rules operate to change the position or the form of the accent. For example, why does the accent of ἄνθρωπος change position when it is in the genitive? (Rules 2 and 3.) Why does νῆσοι have a circumflex? (Rule 4: final -οι is short.)

ἄνθρωπος, ἀνθρώπου, ἄνθρωποι   δοῦλος, δούλου
πλοῖον, πλοίου, πλοῖα   προφήτης, προφῆται
ὁδός, ὁδοί, ὁδοῖς   πρόβατον, προβάτων
σοφῶς, σοφός, σοφοῖς   ἀγορά, ἀγορᾶς
νῆσος, νήσῳ, νῆσοι   τιμή, τιμῆς

Sample Sentences

Read these aloud, noting how the accents are placed. Be sure to stress the syllable on which the accent occurs (whether acute or circumflex).

τὴν δούλην ἐν τῇ ἀγορᾷ εἶδον οὗτοι οἱ σοφοί.

εἶδον αὐτόν, ὁ δὲ οὐκ εἶδεν ἐμέ.

οἱ προφῆται εἶπον τοὺς λόγους ἐν τῇ νήσῳ.

Lesson 1: Exercise in Class

As well as accents, the correct breathings are to be inserted where needed.

1. τον δουλον και τους δουλους, τιμη και λογοι.
2. ειδον την νησον, ουκ ειδον την οδον του προφητου.
3. οι προφηται και οι στρατιωται εν τη νησῳ.
4. της αγορας, του δουλου, τῳ δουλῳ, τα προβατα.
5. του αποστολου, των ανθρωπων, σοφως ειπες ανθρωπε.
6. οι αποστολοι εν τη αγορᾳ ειπον λογους τῳ θεῳ.

Lesson 1: Homework

1. απολυω την δουλην και τους ανθρωπους εκ της νησου.
2. πλοια εχομεν και δουλους εν αυτοις, προβατα ουκ εχομεν.
3. τον κακον προφητην ειδεν ο σοφος ανηρ.
4. εν τῳ κακῳ πλοιῳ φευγουσιν οι καλοι ανθρωποι.
5. εκ των δουλων αλλα ουκ εκ των προβατων ερχονται.
6. εν τη νησῳ θεοι και δουλοι και ναυται αγαθοι.

Verbs

In verbs, the general rule is that the accent is *recessive*, that is, the accent goes as far from the end of the word as possible, within the limits allowed by the basic rules (lesson 1). Most verb forms follow this rule, but there are exceptions.

Recessive

The following are samples of verb forms that have normal recessive accent. The verb λύω is used as the main model, to give an overview of the accent position in the various tenses. Some other verbs are illustrated as well, including some forms showing the recessive accent in compounds. It is suggested you run over these (aloud!), noting where the accent occurs. It may help to have your usual grammar book open beside you, to see the conjugation in full. Remember, these are all recessive, so they are not difficult.

Present tense:

λύω	λύομεν
λύεις	λύετε
λύει	λύουσι

Imperfect, aorist, perfect tenses (first person):

ἔλυον	ἔλυσα	λέλυκα		
ἔλιπον	εἶδον	εἶχον	εἶπον	ἦλθον

Middle/passive forms:

λύομαι	ἐλυόμην	
ἐλυσάμην	ἐλύθην	λέλυμαι

Subjunctives:

λύωσι	λίπω, λίπωσι	λύωμαι	λυθῶ (contracted from -έω)

Infinitives:

λύειν	λύεσθαι	λύσασθαι

Imperatives:

λῦε, λύετε	λάμβανε	σῶσον	λυέτω
λύου	λύθητι		
ἀπόλυε	ἄπελθε	ἀπόλυσον	λίπε

Verbs with first person in -μι ("μι verbs"):

τίθημι	δίδωμι	εἶμι	ἄπειμι

The Exceptions

There are exceptions to the recessive accent in certain **infinitive** and **imperative** forms. This does not mean all infinitives and imperatives are exceptional (as the examples above show).

1. Aorist active **infinitives** in -σαι, accent on second last (though final -αι is short):

> ἀπολῦσαι, παιδεῦσαι, καλέσαι, βαπτίσαι, λῦσαι, πρᾶξαι

> Here also belong infinitives like the following: ἀγγεῖλαι, μεῖναι, ἐγεῖραι[1]

2. All **infinitives** in -ναι, on second last:

> λελυκέναι, λυθῆναι, διδόναι, στῆναι, εἶναι, ἀπεῖναι, ἀπιέναι

3. Second-aorist **infinitives**, on last; second-aorist middle on second last:

> λιπεῖν, ἐλθεῖν, λιπέσθαι, γενέσθαι

4. Perfect middle/passive **infinitives**, on second last:

> λελύσθαι (-ŭ-),[2] βεβλῆσθαι

5. Second-aorist middle **imperatives**, on last:

> λιποῦ, ἀντιλαβοῦ

6. The special five active **imperatives**, on last:

> εἰπέ, ἐλθέ, εὑρέ, ἰδέ, λαβέ

---

1. Historical note: the endings are ultimately derived from -σαι.
2. Note on symbols: ᾰ = short, ᾱ = long.

Plural εἰπέτε, ἐλθέτε, etc.

(But in later Greek: ἴδε, λάβε and ἴδετε, λάβετε.)

Compound Verbs

Special patterns apply to compound verbs, that is, verbs compounded with a preposition (e.g., ἀπολύω).

1. The accent does not precede the *augment* (found in past tenses, indicative):

   ἀπῆν, παρεῖδον, εἰσῆλθον, ἀπεῖπον

   Contrast a normal recessive accent in forms without the augment:

   ἄπειμι, ἔξεστι, ἀπόλυσον, παράλαβε, ἄπειπε (imperative)

2. In aorist imperatives of compound verbs, if it is a *monosyllabic* imperative (e.g., δός), the following patterns are seen:

   ἀπόδος, περίθες, ἄφες, κατάθου, παράσχου, ἐκθοῦ

3. In aorist subjunctives of compound -μι verbs the pattern is: ἀποδῶ

   Participles are treated with adjectives in lesson 5.

Lesson 2: Exercise in Class

1. απολυομεν, απελυσα, απολυσαι (inf.), απολυειν, απολελυμεθα.
2. απολυθηναι, κατεβην, θεασασθαι, ποιησουσιν, εδοξεν.
3. ειναι, εφαινετο, πρεπειν, επεμπον, απηλθεν, εκελευσε, δραμειν.
4. επιμειναι, κελευσαι, εφη, μετεστραφην, ηρομην, προσερχεται.
5. περιμενετε, περιμεινωμεν, δοξετε, δοξαζεις, λελοιπα, επαθετε.
6. ηρξατο λεγειν αυτοις και ειπεν· ιατρε, θεραπευσον σεαυτον.

Lesson 2: Homework

1. οι ανθρωποι απελυοντο, απολελυνται, απελυθησαν, απολυθησονται.
2. επιστελλειν, βαλειν, ειναι, γεγραφεναι, παυεσθαι, ελυομην.
3. χειμων εγενετο και τροφην ουκ ειχον και γυμνοι ησαν, αλλα επετιθεντο.
4. ιδε, οι ναυται ερχονται· αναστηθι και ερχου μετ᾽ αυτων.
5. ουδεις εασει τον δημον πραξαι η αγγειλαι οτι αν βουληται.
6. εδοξεν αναβαλεσθαι εις αλλην εκκλησιαν· ουκετι γαρ ειδον τας χειρας.

Nouns and Adjectives

In nouns, and other words that decline (adjectives, participles, pronouns), each word has its own individual accent. The general rule is that the accent of these words remains in the same position and in the same form (acute or circumflex), unless it is required to change by the basic rules. It returns to its original position whenever it can. A handy term for this is the *home base* of the accent. What the individual accent of a given noun or adjective will be is not always predictable, but there are some common types.

Common Types

The list below consists mostly of nouns, with one adjective. Each group can be recognized by the final element used to form them. All (or nearly all) the formations of the same type have the same accentuation. So, for example, all nouns ending in -ᾰ have a recessive accent. (γλῶσσα has a circumflex in accordance with rule 4.)

-ίᾱ· οἰκία, ἀδικία
-ᾰ· θάλαττα, εὔνοια, ἀλήθεια, δόξα, γλῶσσα

-ις, -σις· πόλις, γένεσις
-μα· ὄνομα, σῶμα, πρᾶγμα
-οσύνη· δικαιοσύνη
-ικός· ναυτικός
-εύς· βασιλεύς
-ότης· δεινότης

There are also many noun and adjective types in which one pattern is usual, with some exceptions. Examples:

δαίμων but ἡγεμών
ἀδικία but στρατιά

Unpredictable

The accent varies in a lot of words that look similar. There is no clear reason for most of them: that's just the way they are. Notice how the accent differs in the following lists, as you read them aloud (from left to right):

ἄνθρωπος	παρθένος	καιρός
πρόβατον	παιδίον	ἱερόν
ἔρημος	φίλος	ἀγαθός
ἄξιος	ἐναντίος	δεξιός
πόλεμος	—	ποταμός
—	πλήρης	ἀληθής

κόσμος	ἀριθμός
διαθήκη	πληγή
γνώμη	τιμή
ἡμέρα	ἀγορά
πολίτης	κριτής
πούς	βοῦς

Standard Declensions

As we did in lesson 2 on verbs, we take some samples of standard nouns and adjectives to remind ourselves of their declension and how the accents are placed. Again, it will be helpful to have your grammar book open, to see the full declension.

First-declension feminine nouns (in -ᾱ, -η, -ᾰ):

χώρα   νίκη   τιμή   θάλαττα, θάλασσα

First-declension masculine nouns (in -ᾱς, -ης):

νεανίας   πολίτης

Second-declension nouns (in -ος, -ον):

ἄνθρωπος   δῶρον
ὁδός   ἱερόν

Second/first-declension adjectives (in -ος, -ᾱ/η, -ον):

ἄξιος, ἀξία, ἄξιον
ἀγαθός, ἀγαθή, ἀγαθόν

ἄδικος, ἄδικον

Third-declension nouns and adjectives:

φύλαξ, φύλακος	ἐλπίς, ἐλπίδος
σῶμα, σώματος	ἀγών, ἀγῶνος
ὕδωρ, ὕδατος	γένος, γένους
βασιλεύς, -έως	πόλις, πόλεως
πατήρ, πάτερ, πατέρα, πατρός, πατρί, . . .	
ἡδύς, ἡδεῖα, ἡδύ	ἀληθής, -ές

In third-declension nouns that are monosyllabic (in the nominative singular) the accent shifts to the **last** syllable in the *genitive and dative*.[1] Example:

πούς, πόδα, ποδός, ποδί   πόδες, πόδας, ποδῶν, ποσί

Note vowel length in accusative plurals in -ας: **first** declension -ᾱς is long, but **third** declension -ᾰς is short: so accent χώρᾱς but ἀγῶνᾰς.

---

1. Historical note: this is related to the change from *acute* in nominative and accusative to *circumflex* in genitive and dative, seen in lesson 1.

Odd or Irregular Declension

A number of nouns and adjectives have oddities in their declension, while following a mainly normal pattern. The only ones you need to notice at this stage are:

γυνή, γυναῖκα, γυναικός, γυναικί
γυναῖκες, γυναῖκας, γυναικῶν, γυναιξί

ἀνήρ, ἄνδρα, ἀνδρός, ἀνδρί
ἄνδρες, ἄνδρας, ἀνδρῶν, ἀνδράσι

πᾶς, πάντα, παντός, παντί
πάντες, πάντας, πάντων, πᾶσι

Lesson 3: Exercise in Class

1. ο αγαθος φιλος, τη αγαθη νικη, τω αδικω πολιτη, του δεξιου ποδος, τους δεξιους ποδας.
2. τα παιδια, τα ονοματα, τας γενεσεις, τας ελπιδας, τους αριθμους.
3. τον πατερα, την μητερα, την γυναικα, τον ανδρα, την γην, τον βουν.
4. εν τω ιερω, εις τας οικιας, εκ της αξιας πολεως, εκ της εναντιας θαλασσης.
5. την δεινοτητα, τον βασιλεα, τη νυκτι, τη ημερᾳ, τους φυλακας.
6. πως δυσκολως οι τα χρηματα εχοντες εις την βασιλειαν του θεου εισελευσονται.

Lesson 3: Homework

1. ευνοια, τραπεζα, πολιτεια, αισχυνη, ευφροσυνη, τιμη και προσκυνησις.
2. τον αγωνα του σωματος, την γενεσιν του κοσμου, τον φιλον των ανθρωπων.
3. τω πατρι, της μητρος, την γυναικα, τον ανδρα, του ποταμου, της αγορας.
4. αιτιος ο ανθρωπος ο μαντικος, οτι την σεμνην θεαν εν τοις θεοις ουκ αισχυνεται.

5. αρετη και δικη, κινδυνος σαφης, πολεμος μικρος, φοβος και μισος, φαντασμα.

6. το μεν πνευμα προθυμον, η δε σαρξ ασθενης.

Good Words to Know

This lesson consists simply of taking you through a list of general vocabulary and "function words" (like the article) that are used constantly in Greek. The aim is to help you become familiar with them, so that you can use them, *and* recognize them, with confidence and without having to check them all the time. Learn them once and for all and you will never go wrong. Reading aloud aids the process.

Demonstratives:

οὗτος, αὕτη, τοῦτο (= "this": note rough breathing)

ἐκεῖνος, ἐκείνη, ἐκεῖνο

ὅδε, ἥδε, τόδε

Article and some pronouns:

ὁ, ἡ, τό (article)

ὅς, ἥ, ὅ (relative pronoun)

αὐτός, αὐτή, αὐτό (= "he, she, it": note differences from οὗτος)

ἀλλήλων

Personal pronouns:

ἐγώ, ἐμέ, ἐμοῦ, ἐμοί   ὑμεῖς, ὑμᾶς, ὑμῶν, ὑμῖν

σύ, σέ, σοῦ, σοί   ἡμεῖς, ἡμᾶς, ἡμῶν, ἡμῖν

Interrogatives:

τίς; τί; (= "who?" "what?": always acute on ί)

πότε; ποῦ; πῶς; πόθεν; ποῖ;

Negatives:

οὐ, οὐκ, οὐχ, μή

οὐδείς, οὐδεμία, οὐδέν

μηδείς, μηδεμία, μηδέν

Conjunctions:

ἐάν, ἄν ("if"); ὡς, εἰ (no accent)

οὐδέ, μηδέ, οὔτε, μήτε, εἴτε

ὅτι, ὅτε, ἐπεί, ἐπειδή

ἵνα, ὅπως, ἕως, πρίν, ὥστε

ἀλλά, ἢ . . . ἤ ("either . . . or")

Prepositions:

εἰς, ἐκ, ἐν (no accent)

πρό, πρός (with accent)

ἀνά, ἀπό, διά, ἐπί, κατά, παρά, περί, ὑπέρ (accent on last)

Particles:

μὲν . . . δὲ . . .

γάρ, οὖν, ἄρα, ἆρα, δή, καίτοι, μέντοι, ἄν

Numeral:

εἷς, μία, ἕν; ἑνός (genitive)

Adverbs:

ἐκεῖ, νῦν, τότε, ἔξω, ἔσω, ἄνω, κάτω

ἔτι, οὐκέτι, μηκέτι

εὖ, μάλα, μᾶλλον, μάλιστα

οἴκαδε, ἐνθάδε, Ἀθήναζε

Common nouns:

ἀδελφός, στρατηγός

δαίμων, ἀγών, ἄρχων

ψυχή, φυλακή, τύχη

πούς, χείρ, παῖς, γῆ, φῶς

Common adjectives:

πολύς, πολλή, πολύ

μέγας, μεγάλη, μέγα

μόνος, φίλος, ὀλίγος, πρῶτος

σοφός, κακός, καλός, δεινός, μικρός, σεμνός, ἱερός

δίκαιος, ἅγιος

ἄλλος, ἕτερος, πᾶς

Lesson 4: Exercise in Class

1. ο αγαθος, την καλην, τω μικρω, τα αγια, μονος αγιος,
   των αλλων, τα ετερα.
2. αι φυλακαι, τους δαιμονας, τους στρατηγους, οι αγωνες,
   οι μεγαλοι, οι αυτοι.
3. τουτω τω αδελφω, ταυτην την τιμην, αυται αι γυναικες,
   των φιλων αυτων.
4. τις σεμνος ανθρωπος; τι τουτο; προς τινα ελεγε ταυτα;
   πως και ποτε ηλθον εκεινοι;
5. ινα ελθη· ει γαρ λεγει· ουτε εμε ουτε σε· αλλα ουδεις
   εκει, πολλοι δε ενθαδε.
6. μη λεγε τουτο το μεγα κακον περι ημων· μαλλον δε
   υμεις φυλαξατε α λεγετε.

Lesson 4: Homework

1. πολεμος ετερος, πληγη αδικος, δικη αλλη, μια οικια,
   κριτης εναντιος, ολιγοι φιλοι.
2. ταυτης δε της δοξης της μεγαλης ου μετεχουσι πολλοι ει
   μη η πολις ημων.
3. τη ημερα εν η εγενετο ουτε μαχη ουτε ναυμαχια κατα
   γην η κατα θαλατταν.
4. τον αυτον αγωνα ουτος ο ανηρ ο δικαιος εδραμεν ως εν
   τω πρωτω χρονω.

5. ηλθον ουν οι αρχιερεις προς τον φυλακα και ειπεν αυτῳ, δια τι ουκ απηγαγες αυτον;

6. ταδε λεγει κυριος· μνησθητι ταυτα, οτι εγω εποιησα την γην και παντα τα επ᾽ αυτης.

More about Nouns and Adjectives

Participles

Participles, though they are part of the verb, also have characteristics of adjectives and are accented like adjectives. That is, the accent of each participle has a "home base" (lesson 3), and it stays there if it can, *within the limits allowed by the basic rules*. This means it may have to change to a different position sometimes. The home base of participles varies. Some forms are recessive, but others are specially marked by the position of their accent.

Recessive

Home base **third last** in middle/passive participles in -όμενος, -άμενος, etc.:

λυόμενος, λυομένη, λυόμενον
λυσάμενος, λυσαμένη, λυσάμενον
λιπόμενος, λιπομένη, λιπόμενον

τιμώμενος, . . .

δεικνύμενος, . . .

ἀποθανούμενος, . . .

Home Base in Special Position

1. Home base **second last** in perfect middle/passive participles in -μένος:

   λελυμένος, λελυμένη, λελυμένον

   τὰ γεγραμμένα

2. Home base **second last** (of nominative masculine singular) in:

   ### Present participle:
   ἀκούων, ἀκούουσα, ἀκοῦον, ἀκούοντος (genitive)

   ### Future:
   λύσων, . . .

   ### First-aorist participle:
   ἀκούσας, ἀκούσασα, ἀκοῦσαν, ἀκούσαντος
   (genitive)

   λύσας, λύσασα, λῦσαν
   (Note length of vowels: -ᾱς, -ᾱσᾰ, -ᾰν)

3. Home base **last** (of nominative masculine singular) in:

Second aorist:

λιπών, λιποῦσα, λιπόν

(But middle λιπόμενος, recessive)

Perfect active:

λελυκώς, λελυκυῖα, λελυκός, λελυκότος (genitive)

εἰδώς, εἰδυῖα, εἰδός

Aorist passive:

λυθείς, λυθεῖσα, λυθέν, λυθέντος (genitive)

Present and aorist active of -μι verbs:

τιθείς, δεικνύς, διδούς

δούς, δόντος (genitive)

ὤν, οὖσα, ὄν

ἰών, ἰοῦσα, ἰόν

Participles in Compounds

The accent behaves as if the word were *not* a compound. That is, the accent of the participle stays on its home base and does not recede to the preposition:

ἀπών, ἀποῦσα, ἀπόν

ἀπιών, ἀπιοῦσα, ἀπιόν, ἀπιόντος (genitive)

ἀναστάς   ἀναβάς   ἀποδούς

ἀπολιπών   ἀπολῦον   τὸ συμφέρον

The Feminine Genitive Plural

The genitive plural of feminine nouns, adjectives, and participles behaves in a special way in regard to accentuation. The reason is historical: the ending -ῶν is contracted from -έων, derived from an older form -άων (found in Homer). The nouns keep the accent where it was originally, that is, on the last syllable, but the adjectives and participles are inconsistent.

1. All **nouns** of the first declension (feminine and masculine): accent on the *last* syllable (-ῶν):

   χώρα, χωρῶν   νίκη, νικῶν
   θάλαττα, θαλαττῶν   δόξα, δοξῶν
   νεανίας, νεανιῶν   πολίτης, πολιτῶν
   κριτής, κριτῶν

2. **Adjectives** and **participles**: some shift the accent to the last, some don't.

   Those in -ος, -η/ᾱ, -ον do not shift:[1]
       δίκαιος, δικαία, δικαίων
       ἄξιος, ἀξία, ἀξίων
       λυόμενος, λυομένη, λυομένων
       αὕτη, τούτων

---

1. Rule of thumb: if feminine genitive plural is the same form as *masculine* genitive plural, no shift of accent: e.g., τούτων is the same in both.

ἐκείνη, ἐκείνων
μεγάλη, μεγάλων

The rest do shift:

μέλαινα, μελαινῶν
ἡδεῖα, ἡδειῶν
λύουσα, λυουσῶν
λύσασα, λυσασῶν
οὖσα, οὐσῶν
πᾶσα, πασῶν (masculine πάντων)

Lesson 5: Exercise in Class

1. λυσας, η λυουσα, οι λυσαντες, της λυουσης, ο απολυσων, ο πραξας, η πραξασα.
2. οι λυομενοι, οι λελυμενοι, τα λελυμενα, τα βεβλημενα, λαβομενος, ωρμημενους.
3. αγοντες, αγαγοντες, δραμοντα, οι απολιποντες, οι ιδοντες, ο αναστας, τιθεις.
4. λελυκυια, τους λελυκοτας, το γεγονος, ειδως, λυθεις, πεμφθεις, τα ποιηθεντα.
5. πολλων πολιτων γεγονοτων δια πολλων ημερων, της τε πολεως εν ταραχη ουσης.
6. του αρχοντος απιοντος εκ των χωρων και κατιδοντος πολλας των μεγαλων οικιων.

Lesson 5: Homework

1. παντων αγοντων, πολλοι αγαγοντες, η δραμουσα, οι απολιποντες, οι ιδοντες.
2. αναβλεψας δε ειδεν τους εισβαλλοντας τα δωρα και χηραν εχουσαν μονον δυο.
3. πασα η γη, παντων και πασων, πολλων δωρων, πρωτος ων, ημερων ουσων.
4. πολλων αποθνησκοντων, επεμψαν πρεσβεις βουλομενοι συμμαχοι ειναι αυτοις.

5. εχοντες, παραδοντας, τα γεγονοτα, πεποιημενος, επιουσα, το εξον.

6. πολιν μεγα αγαθον ειργασμενην εν τοις μεγιστοις κινδυνοις γενομενην.

Contraction

The accentuation of contracted forms is simple. First ask yourself: What was the uncontracted form? Where was its accent? Then choose between the two following alternatives.

Alternative 1: On One of the Contracting Vowels

First, if the accent was on **one of the contracting vowels**, then it will be on the resulting contracted vowel. (It helps to remember that a contracted vowel is always long.) The accent on the contracted vowel is *mostly* a circumflex, but *not always*. There are two possible results:

1. If the accent was on the **first** of the two vowels, the result is a **circumflex**:

   Verbs:
   φιλῶ < φιλέω (< = "derives from")
   τιμῶ < τιμάω
   δηλῶ < δηλόω
   φιλεῖ < φιλέει

τιμᾷ < τιμάει
φιλοῦμεν < φιλέομεν
φιλοῦσι < φιλέουσι
ἐρῶ < ἐρέω
ἀγγελῶ < ἀγγελέω
λυθῶ < λυθέω

Nouns, adjectives:

πλοῦς < πλόος
ἁπλοῦς < ἁπλόος
ἀληθοῦς < ἀληθέος
ἀληθῆ < ἀληθέα
βασιλεῖ < βασιλέ-ι

2. If the accent was on the **second** of the two vowels, the
   result is usually an **acute**, sometimes a circumflex, in
   accordance with the basic rules:

φιλούμενος < φιλεόμενος
ἐποιούμην < ἐποιεόμην
ποιούμεθα < ποιεόμεθα
ἑστῶτες < ἑσταότες ("σωτῆρα rule" applies)

Alternative 2: On Another Vowel

Alternatively, if the accent was on **another vowel**, then it will stay where it was. It is nearly always an **acute**, but a circumflex is possible:

Verbs:
> ἐφίλει < ἐφίλεε
> ἐποίουν < ἐποίεον
> ἐτίμα < ἐτίμαε
> ἑώρα < ἑώραε
> ἐδήλου < ἐδήλοε
> ἐτίμων < ἐτίμαον
> ἑώρων < ἑώραον
> φιλουμένη < φιλεομένη
> ποιουσῶν < ποιεουσῶν

Nouns, adjectives:
> περίπλους < περίπλοος
> εὔνους < εὔνοος
> γένους < γένεος
> γένη < γένεα

Oddities

Exceptions to the normal rules of contraction are sometimes found, as in:

χρυσοῦς, ἀργυροῦς but χρύσεος, ἀργύρεος
ἔκπλους, ἔκπλου (not ἐκπλοῦ < ἐκπλόου)

Lesson 6: Exercise in Class

1. ποιω, ποιουμεν, φιλειτε, εποιουν, εποιουμεν, φιλουμαι, φιλειται, ποιουμενη.
2. τιμω, τιμα, τιμας, ετιμων, ετιμα, δηλω, δηλοι, δηλουσι, εδηλου, επλεον.
3. ερουσιν, αγγελω, βαλω, αποθανουμαι, μενετε, μενειτε, εμεινατε.
4. του γενους, το αληθες, τα αληθη, τον πλουν, εις πολλα ετη, νους, ανοια, ευνους.
5. αγαπατε αλληλους, προσεκυνει αυτω, τιμα τον πατερα, ορα μη ειπης.
6. τους φιλουντας ημας, το επιμελεισθαι της χωρας, ινα απολυθωσιν οι ανδρες.

Lesson 6: Homework

1. οι ποιουντες ταυτα ου ποιουσι τα ποιουμενα υπο των φιλουντων τα αγαθα.
2. οραν, ποιειν, ορασθαι, ποιεισθαι, τιμωμεν, φιλουμεν, ορωντες, βοηθουντων.
3. φοβουμαι, φοβουμενοι, μισω, εμισουν, εμισησα, αγαπα, ηγαπα, ηγαπησε.
4. το πλοιον το χρυσουν, νους ασθενης, καρδιαι αληθεις, βασιλεις δικαιοι.

5. αποστελουσιν τας ναυς, κρινειτε τους πολιτας,
   αποθανουνται τη αυτη ημερα.

6. ινα λυθω, ινα ποιωμεν, πιπτω, πεσουμαι, επεσον,
   πεπτωκα.

LESSON 7

Enclitics

Enclitics are a special group of words that are unemphatic and unaccented. While unaccented themselves, they usually have an effect on the accentuation of the preceding word. The patterns of accentuation are largely (but not entirely) explained if the enclitic is thought of as combined with the preceding word. Thus a combination like ἄνθρωπος + μου requires another stress somewhere in addition to the normal accent of ἄνθρωπος: on -ος is where it has to be. In pronunciation, stress *both* accented syllables in ἄνθρωπός μου, but only the *first* in δῶρόν μου.

The Enclitics

This is a list of the main enclitics. Note that many have an accented alternative with a difference of meaning. Two verbs, εἰμί and φημί (and only these two), are enclitic in most of their forms.

1. με, μου, μοι   σε, σου, σοι (note: *not* ἐγώ, σύ)

   = the unemphatic forms of first- and second-person singular pronouns

(The emphatic forms are: ἐμέ, ἐμοῦ, ἐμοί and σέ, σοῦ, σοί)

2. τις, τι all forms = "someone," "something"

(Alternative with accent, always acute: interrogative τίς; τί; = "who?" "what?")

3. που, ποτε, πως, ποθεν, ποι = "somewhere," etc.

(Alternative with accent: interrogative ποῦ; πότε; πῶς; πόθεν; ποῖ; = "where?" etc.)

4. εἰμι, ἐστι, ἐσμεν, ἐστε, εἰσι (*not* second-person εἶ)

(ἔστι is sometimes not enclitic: see lesson 8)

5. φημι, φησι, φαμεν, φατε, φασι (*not* second-person φής)

6. Particles: γε, περ, τε, τοι

The Patterns of Accentuation

These are all the patterns that can occur. In the first column are the combinations with a *monosyllabic* enclitic (μου), in the second those with a *disyllabic* enclitic (ἐστιν). Saying them aloud will help you remember them.

1	ἀδελφός μου	ἀδελφός ἐστιν	Preceding word keeps acute
2	ἄνθρωπός μου	ἄνθρωπός ἐστιν	Preceding word gets extra acute
3	λόγος μου	λόγος ἐστὶν . . . / ἐστίν.	Disyllabic enclitic gets extra accent
4		λόγων τινῶν	*ditto*, circumflex only here
5	φῶς μου	φῶς ἐστιν	No change; *not* φῶς ἐστίν
6	δῶρόν μου	δῶρόν ἐστιν	Preceding word gets extra acute

Unemphatic versus Emphatic

Notice the difference in meaning between an unemphatic enclitic and the accented, emphatic form of the same word, as in these examples:

εἶδέν με / εἶδεν ἐμέ ("he saw me / he saw *me*")

πρός σε / πρὸς σέ ("to you / to *you*")

ἔρχεταί τις / τίς ἔρχεται; ("someone is coming / who is coming?")

Succession of Enclitics

If more than one enclitic occurs in succession, an enclitic transfers its accent to the preceding enclitic (which transfers *its* accent to the preceding word). Example:

εἴ τίς τι εἶπεν (= "if anyone said anything")

Note that τίς, though it has an accent here, still means "anyone," *not* "who?"

Proclitics

A "proclitic" is a word without an accent of its own, adhering closely to the following word. Examples of common proclitics are ὁ, εἰ, εἰς, ἐν, οὐ, ὡς. They only acquire an accent in cases like εἴ τίς τι above, where εἰ receives an accent from τις.

More Illustrations of Enclitics

ἦσάν ποτε
ἦν ποτε
ὀλίγοι τινές
τὸ ὄνομά μου
πολλοί ἐσμεν
μέγας ἐστίν

Lesson 7: Exercise in Class

1. δουλος εστι, αποστολος εστι, αποστολοι εισιν, αγαθοι
   εισι, δικαιος ειμι.
2. ειπον τινες, ανθρωπος τις, αποστολος τις, πραγμα τι,
   λογος τις, ολιγα τινα.
3. τουτο το ονομα μου· τι το ονομα σου; το ονομα αυτου
   εστιν· τι λεγεις;
4. ηλθον ποτε ανδρες τινες προς πολιν τινα, και ελεγον
   πολιταις τισιν· που εσμεν;
5. κατα τε γην και κατα θαλατταν, ουτε μαχη ουτε
   ναυμαχια, γυναικες τε και ανδρες.
6. συ ουκ εχεις τι λεγειν· ημεις φαμεν αλλ υμεις ουκ
   αποκρινεσθε ποτε.

Lesson 7: Homework

1. τον πεμψαντα με· αποστολοι τινες· φως εστι του
   κοσμου· φως του κοσμου εστιν.
2. ειπε μοι το ονομα σου· τι γαρ; ονομα τι ουκ εχεις; πως
   εστιν; ουδεν λεγεις μοι;
3. τηρησατε τας εντολας μου, λαε μου· τιμα τον πατερα
   σου και την μητερα σου.
4. εγω μεν σε ειδον, συ δε εμε ουκ ειδες, και το δωρον μου
   ουκ εδωκας μοι.

5. λεγουσιν τινες παλιν, τι συ λεγεις περι αυτου, οτι ηνεῳξεν σου τους οφθαλμους;

6. συ γε ουκ εχεις τι φαναι ει μη ρημα τι μικρον τε και αδικον.

LESSON 8

Scaling the Heights

In this final lesson we gather a miscellany of additional features for those who are ready to go a step further. Some are fairly routine, others more challenging, but all are useful to add to one's store of knowledge if possible. This list covers a lot, but not everything.

Optative

The optative third-person endings in -οι, -αι are *long*:

ἀπολύοι, λαμβάνοι, παιδεύσαι[1]

So three forms that look the same are distinguished by their accent:

ἀπολῦσαι = aorist active infinitive (-αι short, accent of infinitive stays on second last)

---

1. Note that -αι = alternative ending to -ειε.

ἀπολύσαι = aorist active **optative** third-person singular (-αι *long*)

ἀπόλυσαι = aorist middle imperative (-αι short, accent recessive)

More on Enclitics

There are some more points to notice about the behaviour of εἰμι and φημι:

The form ἐστι is non-enclitic and accented ἔστι when:

It begins a sentence or clause.
It expresses existence or possibility.
It follows οὐκ, μή, εἰ, ὡς, καί, ἀλλά, ἀλλ'.
Examples:
οὐκ ἔστιν, ἔστι πόλις, εἰ ἔστι

Other parts of εἰμι (also φημι) accent the *last* syllable in those cases.

Examples:
οὐκ εἰμί, οὐκ εἰσίν, οὐκ ἐστέ, εἰμὶ ἐγώ, ἀλλ' εἰσίν
φημὶ γάρ, φησίν, καὶ φησίν·

Other Enclitics

Here are some additional enclitics that may be encountered, mainly in poetry:

ἑ, οὑ, οἱ, μιν, νιν, σφε, νυν

Various Tricks

Verbs:

ἔξεστι but ἐξέσται, ἀπέσται

ἔνι = ἔνεστι

πρόσχωμεν, σχῶμεν, ἀφῖγμαι

Elisions:

φήμ’ ἐγώ (for φημὶ ἐγώ)

ταῦτ’ ἐστί (for ταῦτά ἐστι)

πόλλ’ ἔπαθον (for πολλὰ ἔπαθον)

ἄνθρωπός τ’

Miscellaneous:

μία, μιᾶς, μιᾷ (shift like a third-declension monosyllable)

ἡδίων, ἥδιον

αὐτάρκης, αὔταρκες

ὦ, ὤ

οὐ, οὔ

οὐχί, μήτι

κῆρυξ τις (not κῆρύξ τις)
οὔκουν ("not then"), οὐκοῦν ("so then")
ὅστις, οὗτινος, ᾧτινι, etc. (= relative pronoun + τις)
οὑτοσί, ταυτί ("deictic" iota)

Genitive-Plural Exceptions

The accent is usually on the last syllable (-ῶν) in the genitive plural of third-declension monosyllables (lesson 3), but there are some notable exceptions:

παίδων, φώτων, ὤτων, πάντων (plus a few others)

Vocatives

Some have a recessive accent, as in:

ἄδελφε, δέσποτα, σῶτερ, Σώκρατες

Rule Violation Explained

Derivation from an earlier form explains the violation of rule 2 in:

πόλεως (< -ηος), πολίτεω (< -ηο)

More Symbols

Diaeresis to separate vowels: ἀΐδιος, βοΐ, εὐνοϊκῶς, πραΰς, πρωΐ . . .

Coronis to mark crasis: κἀγώ, τοὔνομα, ἄνθρωπος
(< ὁ ἄνθρωπος)

Iota adscript: if present, the accent is written on the *first* vowel:

-ᾱι, -ῃι, -ωι (as if -ᾳ, -ῃ, -ῳ)
Ἅιδης (as if ᾅδης)
ἀποθνήισκω (as if -θνήισκω)

Position of Accent

A shift of position signals a difference in function or meaning in cases like these:

Anastrophe: if a disyllabic preposition *follows* the word it governs, its accent is on the first syllable:[2]

ἄπο, πάρα, etc. Homeric examples: σαυτῆς πέρι φρόντιζ'; ὁδῷ ἔπι

---

2. Historical note: this is the original position of the accent of these prepositions.

Active and passive meaning: λιθοβόλος (active), ἔκβολος (passive)

Noun and adjective: δόξα, ἔνδοξος; περιβολή, περίβολος

Greek Dialects

Epic dialect has many peculiarities. Here are some samples:

Πηληιάδεω Ἀχιλῆος
πολέμοιο κακοῖο
ἔμμεναι
εἰπέμεν
ἠώς
πάϊς
ἐΰ
Ἀΐδης
φάτο (= ἔφατο), βῆν (= ἔβην), κάτεχε (= κατεῖχε)

In the Lesbian dialect, the recessive accent is general, not just in verbs. Examples:

γύναικες, θέοισιν, χαλέπαν

Lesson 8: Exercise in Class

1. εις το ακουσαι· ουκ εστιν ανθρωπος τις εκει· εξεστι σοι αλλ ουκ εξεσται ποιησαι.

2. ει τουτο πιστευοι, ειποι αν πασιν. ουδεν γαρ τοι αξιον της πολεως πεποιηκε.

3. τουνομα τουτο· εν μια των ημερων· αναστηθι, κυριε, σωσον με, ο θεος μου.

4. τουτι δη εστι παντων χαλεπωτατον πεισαι τινας υμων, ω ανδρες Αθηναιοι.

5. αμεινον εστι σωμα γ᾽ η ψυχην νοσειν. απαν θεου μοι δωμ᾽, ιν᾽ αν λαβη μ᾽ υπνος.

6. αλλ᾽, ω Σωκρατες, το σον τι εστι πραγμα; ποθεν αι διαβολαι σοι αυται γεγονασιν;

Lesson 8: Homework

1. φημι γαρ, ω ανδρες, οι εμε απεκτονατε, τιμωριαν υμιν ηξειν ευθυς.

2. αξιω και δεομαι υμων ευνοικως ακουσαι μου περι ων πεπονθα λεγοντος.

3. τυφλος τα τ᾽ ωτα τον τε νουν τα τ᾽ ομματ᾽ ει.

4. κουδεις γε μ᾽ αν πεισειεν ανθρωπων το μη ουκ ελθειν επ᾽ εκεινον.

5. ποτερον εις Αιδου κατω; και νη Δι᾽ ει τι γ᾽ εστιν ετι κατωτερω.

6. Αχιλληος λαβε γουνατα και κυσε χειρας δεινας ανδροφονους.

Further Practice

Further Practice 1

1. αγγελουσι, επηρωτα, εφιλουν, ερεις, δηλουμεν, επιζητει.
2. το συμφερον τη πολει, του παροντος αιωνος, πολλα παθων.
3. εξηλθον, συνειχον, ινα ιδω, ινα ειδω, ινα η, ινα αποδωμεν.
4. γεγραμμενων, ειδοτα, πεποιηκως, φυγων, μισουμενοι, ελθων.
5. θεασασθαι, δουναι, απιεναι, γενεσθαι, ποιησαι, πεποιησθαι.
6. μηκετι ελθε· περιβαλου το ιματιον· ευλογησαι σε κυριος.

Further Practice 2

1. ουδεις ιππος εν τῳ ποταμῳ ει μη ιπποποταμος, υδατι οντι.
2. τις αρα ουτος εστιν; ο ποιμην ο καλος εκεινος η ετερος τις;
3. των παιδων ευ εχοντων· κυνος εισιοντος· εκ πολεων τινων.

4. αι νηες ουν εις τον λιμενα εισεδεχθησαν υπο των πολιτων.

5. ω ανερ, εστι πασι μια χειρ και εις πους εν τηδε τη ζωη;

6. υιος αγαπητος· ο μαθητης ο ηγαπημενος· αδελφοι πιστοι.

Further Practice 3

1. η δε της βουλης γνωμη ην μια ψηφω απαντας κρινειν τους ανδρας.

2. κατεψηφισαντο των στρατηγων οκτω οντων, απεθανον δε οι παροντες εξ.

3. υστερον δε στασεως τινος γενομενης, απεδρασαν ουτοι πριν κριθηναι.

4. εθη α ουκ εξεστιν ημιν παραδεχεσθαι Ρωμαιοις ουσιν.

5. ιδοντες ειλκυσαν αυτους εις την αγοραν επι τους αρχοντας.

6. πολλας τε επιθεντες αυτοις πληγας, εβαλον εις φυλακην.

Further Practice 4

την μεν παρασκευην, ω ανδρες, και την προθυμιαν των εχθρων των εμων, ωστ᾽ εμε κακως ποιειν εκ παντος τροπου, και δικαιως και αδικως, εξ αρχης επειδη ταχιστα αφικομην εις την πολιν ταυτηνι, σχεδον τι παντες επιστασθε, και ουδεν δει περι τουτων πολλους λογους ποιεισθαι. εγω δε, ω ανδρες,

δεησομαι υμων δικαια και υμιν τε ρᾳδια χαριζεσθαι και εμοι
αξια πολλου τυχειν παρ᾽ υμων.

Further Practice 5

Σωκρατη φησιν αδικειν τους τε νεους διαφθειροντα και θεους
ους η πολις νομιζει ου νομιζοντα, ετερα δε δαιμονια καινα. το
μεν δη εγκλημα τοιουτον εστιν· τουτου δε του εγκληματος
εν εκαστον εξετασωμεν. Φησι γαρ δη τους νεους αδικειν με
διαφθειροντα. εγω δε γε, ω ανδρες Αθηναιοι, αδικειν φημι
Μελητον. . . . Και μοι δευρο, ω Μελητε, ειπε· αλλο τι η περι
πλειστου ποιῃ οπως ως βελτιστοι οι νεωτεροι εσονται; Εγωγε.
Ιθι δη νυν ειπε τουτοις, τις αυτους βελτιους ποιει;

Further Practice 6

τῃ δε μιᾳ των σαββατων ορθρου βαθεως επι το μνημα
ηλθον φερουσαι α ητοιμασαν αρωματα. ευρον δε τον λιθον
αποκεκυλισμενον απο του μνημειου, εισελθουσαι δε ουχ ευρον
το σωμα του κυριου Ιησου. και εγενετο εν τῳ απορεισθαι αυτας
περι τουτου και ιδου ανδρες δυο επεστησαν αυταις εν εσθητι
αστραπτουσῃ. εμφοβων δε γενομενων αυτων και κλινουσων τα
προσωπα εις την γην ειπαν προς αυτας· τι ζητειτε τον ζωντα
μετα των νεκρων; ουκ εστιν ωδε, αλλα ηγερθη.

Bibliography

For comprehensive coverage of accents there are the reference books of Chandler, Bally, and Probert (2003). These are recommended for any further checking of details and an insight into theory. Probert's 2003 work is especially useful for presenting the current state of the discussion of problems, with very full bibliography. It also includes exercises, but is not an easy tool for beginners. Probert's 2006 work is for advanced students.

Goodwin and Smyth are the standard reference grammars. While they do contain all the rules about accentuation, the material is scattered and difficult for the learner to use. But they are the best books to consult for an authoritative presentation of declensions and conjugations.

Bodoh, Marinone, and Patakis provide exhaustive lists of verb forms and principal parts.

A very formal, concise, and rule-based approach, with exercises, is offered in Koster's small work.

Carson's book caters primarily for students of New Testament Greek. It offers 37 lessons, with exercises, and includes full declensions and conjugations as well. There is an emphasis on the build-up of rules, an approach that may not suit everyone.

Bally, Charles. *Manuel d'accentuation grecque.* Berne: Francke, 1945. Repr., 1997.

Bodoh, J. J., et al. *An Index of Greek Verb Forms.* Hildesheim: Olms, 1970.

Carson, D. A. *Greek Accents: A Student's Manual.* Grand Rapids: Baker, 1985.

Chandler, H. W. *A Practical Introduction to Greek Accentuation.* 2nd ed. Oxford: Clarendon, 1881. Repr., 1983.

Goodwin, W. W. *A Greek Grammar.* London: Macmillan, 1894.

Koster, A. J. *A Practical Guide for the Writing of the Greek Accents.* Leiden: Brill, 1962. Repr., 1976.

Marinone, N. *All the Greek Verbs / Tutti i verbi greci.* London: Duckworth, 1985.

Πατάκης, Σ. Α., and Ν. Ε. Τζιράκης. Λεξικό ρημάτων αρχαίας Ελληνικής. Αθήνα: Πατάκη, 1984.

Probert, Philomen. *Ancient Greek Accentuation: Synchronic Patterns, Frequency Effects, and Prehistory.* Oxford: Oxford University Press, 2006.

———. *A New Short Guide to the Accentuation of Ancient Greek.* London: Bristol Classical Press, 2003. [A revision of J. P. Postgate's *A Short Guide to the Accentuation of Ancient Greek* (1924).]

Smyth, H. W. *Greek Grammar.* Rev. by G. M. Messing. Cambridge: Harvard University Press, 1956.

Traditional Accent Terminology

Cf. Probert, *New Short Guide*, §34; Smyth, *Greek Grammar*, §157.

Greek	English	Meaning	Example
τόνος	accent, tone		
ὀξεῖα	acute		ά
βαρεῖα	grave		ὰ
περισπωμένη	circumflex		ᾶ, ᾶ
ὀξύτονος	oxytone	With acute on final syllable	θεός
βαρύτονος	barytone	Not accented on the final syllable	τόνος
περισπώμενος	perispom-enon	With circumflex on final syllable	καλῶς
παροξύτονος	paroxytone	With acute on penultimate syllable	προφήτης
προπερισ-πώμενος	properis-pomenon	With circumflex on penultimate syllable	σωτῆρα

προπαρο-ξύτονος	propar-oxytone	With acute on the antepenultimate syllable	ἀπόστολος
ὀρθότονος	orthotone	In ref. to enclitic: with accent retained	ἔστι
ἐγκλιτική	enclitic	Type of word without accent, attached closely to preceding word	τις
[προκλιτική]	proclitic	Type of word without accent, attached closely to following word	εἰς
ἀναστροφή	anastrophe	Shift of accent of disyllabic preposition from last to first syllable	δόμων ἄπο
πνεῦμα	breathing		
ψιλή	smooth		ἀ
δασεῖα	rough		ἁ

Notes

The noun "understood" with ὀξεῖα, βαρεῖα, περισπωμένη is προσῳδία.

The terms ὀξύτονος, etc., often appear as (τὰ) ὀξύτονα, etc., describing the group.

The Greek terms entered English through Latin, translated or Anglicized.

Answers to Exercises

Lesson 1: Exercise in Class

1. τὸν δοῦλον καὶ τοὺς δούλους, τιμὴ καὶ λόγοι.
2. εἶδον τὴν νῆσον, οὐκ εἶδον τὴν ὁδὸν τοῦ προφήτου.
3. οἱ προφῆται καὶ οἱ στρατιῶται ἐν τῇ νήσῳ.
4. τῆς ἀγορᾶς, τοῦ δούλου, τῷ δούλῳ, τὰ πρόβατα.
5. τοῦ ἀποστόλου, τῶν ἀνθρώπων, σοφῶς εἶπες ἄνθρωπε.
6. οἱ ἀπόστολοι ἐν τῇ ἀγορᾷ εἶπον λόγους τῷ θεῷ.

Lesson 1: Homework

1. ἀπολύω τὴν δούλην καὶ τοὺς ἀνθρώπους ἐκ τῆς νήσου.
2. πλοῖα ἔχομεν καὶ δούλους ἐν αὐτοῖς, πρόβατα οὐκ
   ἔχομεν.
3. τὸν κακὸν προφήτην εἶδεν ὁ σοφὸς ἀνήρ.
4. ἐν τῷ κακῷ πλοίῳ φεύγουσιν οἱ καλοὶ ἄνθρωποι.
5. ἐκ τῶν δούλων ἀλλὰ οὐκ ἐκ τῶν προβάτων ἔρχονται.
6. ἐν τῇ νήσῳ θεοὶ καὶ δοῦλοι καὶ ναῦται ἀγαθοί.

Lesson 2: Exercise in Class

1. ἀπολύομεν, ἀπέλυσα, ἀπολῦσαι, ἀπολύειν, ἀπολελύμεθα.
2. ἀπολυθῆναι, κατέβην, θεάσασθαι, ποιήσουσιν, ἔδοξεν.
3. εἶναι, ἐφαίνετο, πρέπειν, ἔπεμπον, ἀπῆλθεν, ἐκέλευσε, δραμεῖν.
4. ἐπιμεῖναι, κελεῦσαι, ἔφη, μετεστράφην, ἠρόμην, προσέρχεται.
5. περιμένετε, περιμείνωμεν, δόξετε, δοξάζεις, λέλοιπα, ἐπάθετε.
6. ἤρξατο λέγειν αὐτοῖς καὶ εἶπεν· ἰατρέ, θεράπευσον σεαυτόν.

Lesson 2: Homework

1. οἱ ἄνθρωποι ἀπελύοντο, ἀπολέλυνται, ἀπελύθησαν, ἀπολυθήσονται.
2. ἐπιστέλλειν, βαλεῖν, εἶναι, γεγραφέναι, παύεσθαι, ἐλυόμην.
3. χειμὼν ἐγένετο καὶ τροφὴν οὐκ εἶχον καὶ γυμνοὶ ἦσαν, ἀλλὰ ἐπετίθεντο.
4. ἰδέ, οἱ ναῦται ἔρχονται· ἀνάστηθι καὶ ἔρχου μετ᾿ αὐτῶν.
5. οὐδεὶς ἐάσει τὸν δῆμον πρᾶξαι ἢ ἀγγεῖλαι ὅτι ἂν βούληται.
6. ἔδοξεν ἀναβαλέσθαι εἰς ἄλλην ἐκκλησίαν· οὐκέτι γὰρ εἶδον τὰς χεῖρας.

Lesson 3: Exercise in Class

1. ὁ ἀγαθὸς φίλος, τῇ ἀγαθῇ νίκῃ, τῷ ἀδίκῳ πολίτῃ, τοῦ δεξιοῦ ποδός, τοὺς δεξιοὺς πόδας.
2. τὰ παιδία, τὰ ὀνόματα, τὰς γενέσεις, τὰς ἐλπίδας, τοὺς ἀριθμούς.
3. τὸν πατέρα, τὴν μητέρα, τὴν γυναῖκα, τὸν ἄνδρα, τὴν γῆν, τὸν βοῦν.
4. ἐν τῷ ἱερῷ, εἰς τὰς οἰκίας, ἐκ τῆς ἀξίας πόλεως, ἐκ τῆς ἐναντίας θαλάσσης.
5. τὴν δεινότητα, τὸν βασιλέα, τῇ νυκτί, τῇ ἡμέρᾳ, τοὺς φύλακας.
6. πῶς δυσκόλως οἱ τὰ χρήματα ἔχοντες εἰς τὴν βασιλείαν τοῦ θεοῦ εἰσελεύσονται.

(6: NT, *Mark* 10:23.)

Lesson 3: Homework

1. εὔνοια, τράπεζα, πολιτεία, αἰσχύνη, εὐφροσύνη, τιμὴ καὶ προσκύνησις.
2. τὸν ἀγῶνα τοῦ σώματος, τὴν γένεσιν τοῦ κόσμου, τὸν φίλον τῶν ἀνθρώπων.
3. τῷ πατρί, τῆς μητρός, τὴν γυναῖκα, τὸν ἄνδρα, τοῦ ποταμοῦ, τῆς ἀγορᾶς.

4. αἴτιος ὁ ἄνθρωπος ὁ μαντικός, ὅτι τὴν σεμνὴν θεὰν ἐν τοῖς θεοῖς οὐκ αἰσχύνεται.

5. ἀρετὴ καὶ δίκη, κίνδυνος σαφής, πόλεμος μικρός, φόβος καὶ μῖσος, φάντασμα.

6. τὸ μὲν πνεῦμα πρόθυμον, ἡ δὲ σὰρξ ἀσθενής.

(6: NT, *Mark* 14:38.)

Lesson 4: Exercise in Class

1. ὁ ἀγαθός, τὴν καλήν, τῷ μικρῷ, τὰ ἅγια, μόνος ἅγιος, τῶν ἄλλων, τὰ ἕτερα.

2. αἱ φυλακαί, τοὺς δαίμονας, τοὺς στρατηγούς, οἱ ἀγῶνες, οἱ μεγάλοι, οἱ αὐτοί.

3. τούτῳ τῷ ἀδελφῷ, ταύτην τὴν τιμήν, αὗται αἱ γυναῖκες, τῶν φίλων αὐτῶν.

4. τίς σεμνὸς ἄνθρωπος; τί τοῦτο; πρὸς τίνα ἔλεγε ταῦτα; πῶς καὶ πότε ἦλθον ἐκεῖνοι;

5. ἵνα ἔλθῃ· εἰ γὰρ λέγει· οὔτε ἐμὲ οὔτε σέ· ἀλλὰ οὐδεὶς ἐκεῖ, πολλοὶ δὲ ἐνθάδε.

6. μὴ λέγε τοῦτο τὸ μέγα κακὸν περὶ ἡμῶν· μᾶλλον δὲ ὑμεῖς φυλάξατε ἃ λέγετε.

Lesson 4: Homework

1. πόλεμος ἕτερος, πληγὴ ἄδικος, δίκη ἄλλη, μία οἰκία, κριτὴς ἐναντίος, ὀλίγοι φίλοι.

2. ταύτης δὲ τῆς δόξης τῆς μεγάλης οὐ μετέχουσι πολλοὶ εἰ μὴ ἡ πόλις ἡμῶν.

3. τῇ ἡμέρᾳ ἐν ᾗ ἐγένετο οὔτε μάχη οὔτε ναυμαχία κατὰ γῆν ἢ κατὰ θάλατταν.

4. τὸν αὐτὸν ἀγῶνα οὗτος ὁ ἀνὴρ ὁ δίκαιος ἔδραμεν ὡς ἐν τῷ πρώτῳ χρόνῳ.

5. ἦλθον οὖν οἱ ἀρχιερεῖς πρὸς τὸν φύλακα καὶ εἶπεν αὐτῷ, διὰ τί οὐκ ἀπήγαγες αὐτόν;

6. τάδε λέγει κύριος· μνήσθητι ταῦτα, ὅτι ἐγὼ ἐποίησα τὴν γῆν καὶ πάντα τὰ ἐπ᾽ αὐτῆς.

Lesson 5: Exercise in Class

1. λύσας, ἡ λύουσα, οἱ λύσαντες, τῆς λυούσης, ὁ ἀπολύσων, ὁ πράξας, ἡ πράξασα.

2. οἱ λυόμενοι, οἱ λελυμένοι, τὰ λελυμένα, τὰ βεβλημένα, λαβόμενος, ὡρμημένους.

3. ἄγοντες, ἀγαγόντες, δραμόντα, οἱ ἀπολιπόντες, οἱ ἰδόντες, ὁ ἀναστάς, τιθείς.

4. λελυκυῖα, τοὺς λελυκότας, τὸ γεγονός, εἰδώς, λυθείς, πεμφθείς, τὰ ποιηθέντα.

5. πολλῶν πολιτῶν γεγονότων διὰ πολλῶν ἡμερῶν, τῆς τε πόλεως ἐν ταραχῇ οὔσης.

6. τοῦ ἄρχοντος ἀπιόντος ἐκ τῶν χωρῶν καὶ κατιδόντος πολλὰς τῶν μεγάλων οἰκιῶν.

Lesson 5: Homework

1. πάντων ἀγόντων, πολλοὶ ἀγαγόντες, ἡ δραμοῦσα, οἱ ἀπολιπόντες, οἱ ἰδόντες.

2. ἀναβλέψας δὲ εἶδεν τοὺς εἰσβάλλοντας τὰ δῶρα καὶ χήραν ἔχουσαν μόνον δύο.

3. πᾶσα ἡ γῆ, πάντων καὶ πασῶν, πολλῶν δώρων, πρῶτος ὤν, ἡμερῶν οὐσῶν.

4. πολλῶν ἀποθνησκόντων, ἔπεμψαν πρέσβεις βουλόμενοι σύμμαχοι εἶναι αὐτοῖς.

5. ἔχοντες, παραδόντας, τὰ γεγονότα, πεποιημένος, ἐπιοῦσα, τὸ ἐξόν.

6. πόλιν μέγα ἀγαθὸν εἰργασμένην ἐν τοῖς μεγίστοις κινδύνοις γενομένην.

Lesson 6: Exercise in Class

1. ποιῶ, ποιοῦμεν, φιλεῖτε, ἐποίουν, ἐποιοῦμεν, φιλοῦμαι, φιλεῖται, ποιουμένη.

2. τιμῶ, τιμᾷ, τιμᾷς, ἐτίμων, ἐτίμα, δηλῶ, δηλοῖ, δηλοῦσι, ἐδήλου, ἔπλεον.

3. ἐροῦσιν, ἀγγελῶ, βαλῶ, ἀποθανοῦμαι, μένετε, μενεῖτε, ἐμείνατε.

4. τοῦ γένους, τὸ ἀληθές, τὰ ἀληθῆ, τὸν πλοῦν, εἰς πολλὰ ἔτη, νοῦς, ἄνοια, εὔνους.

5. ἀγαπᾶτε ἀλλήλους, προσεκύνει αὐτῷ, τίμα τὸν πατέρα, ὅρα μὴ εἴπῃς.

6. τοὺς φιλοῦντας ἡμᾶς, τὸ ἐπιμελεῖσθαι τῆς χώρας, ἵνα ἀπολυθῶσιν οἱ ἄνδρες.

Lesson 6: Homework

1. οἱ ποιοῦντες ταῦτα οὐ ποιοῦσι τὰ ποιούμενα ὑπὸ τῶν φιλούντων τὰ ἀγαθά.

2. ὁρᾶν, ποιεῖν, ὁρᾶσθαι, ποιεῖσθαι, τιμῶμεν, φιλοῦμεν, ὁρῶντες, βοηθούντων.

3. φοβοῦμαι, φοβούμενοι, μισῶ, ἐμίσουν, ἐμίσησα, ἀγαπᾷ, ἠγάπα, ἠγάπησε.

4. τὸ πλοῖον τὸ χρυσοῦν, νοῦς ἀσθενής, καρδίαι ἀληθεῖς, βασιλεῖς δίκαιοι.

5. ἀποστελοῦσιν τὰς ναῦς, κρινεῖτε τοὺς πολίτας, ἀποθανοῦνται τῇ αὐτῇ ἡμέρᾳ.

6. ἵνα λυθῶ, ἵνα ποιῶμεν, πίπτω, πεσοῦμαι, ἔπεσον, πέπτωκα.

Lesson 7: Exercise in Class

1. δοῦλός ἐστι, ἀπόστολός ἐστι, ἀπόστολοί εἰσιν, ἀγαθοί
   εἰσι, δίκαιός εἰμι.
2. εἶπόν τινες, ἄνθρωπός τις, ἀπόστολός τις, πρᾶγμά τι,
   λόγος τις, ὀλίγα τινά.
3. τοῦτο τὸ ὄνομά μου· τί τὸ ὄνομά σου; τὸ ὄνομα αὐτοῦ
   ἐστιν· τί λέγεις;
4. ἦλθόν ποτε ἄνδρες τινὲς πρὸς πόλιν τινά, καὶ ἔλεγον
   πολίταις τισίν· ποῦ ἐσμεν;
5. κατά τε γῆν καὶ κατὰ θάλατταν, οὔτε μάχη οὔτε
   ναυμαχία, γυναῖκές τε καὶ ἄνδρες.
6. σὺ οὐκ ἔχεις τι λέγειν· ἡμεῖς φαμεν ἀλλ᾽ ὑμεῖς οὐκ
   ἀποκρίνεσθέ ποτε.

Lesson 7: Homework

1. τὸν πέμψαντά με· ἀπόστολοί τινες· φῶς ἐστι τοῦ
   κόσμου· φῶς τοῦ κόσμου ἐστίν.
2. εἰπέ μοι τὸ ὄνομά σου· τί γάρ; ὄνομά τι οὐκ ἔχεις; πῶς
   ἐστιν; οὐδὲν λέγεις μοι;
3. τηρήσατε τὰς ἐντολάς μου, λαέ μου· τίμα τὸν πατέρα
   σου καὶ τὴν μητέρα σου.
4. ἐγὼ μὲν σὲ εἶδον, σὺ δὲ ἐμὲ οὐκ εἶδες, καὶ τὸ δῶρόν μου
   οὐκ ἔδωκάς μοι.

5. λέγουσίν τινες πάλιν, τί σὺ λέγεις περὶ αὐτοῦ, ὅτι
ἠνέῳξέν σου τοὺς ὀφθαλμούς;
6. σύ γε οὐκ ἔχεις τι φάναι εἰ μὴ ῥῆμά τι μικρόν τε καὶ
ἄδικον.

(5: cf. NT, *John* 9:17.)

Lesson 8: Exercise in Class

1. εἰς τὸ ἀκοῦσαι· οὐκ ἔστιν ἄνθρωπός τις ἐκεῖ· ἔξεστί σοι
ἀλλ᾽ οὐκ ἐξέσται ποιῆσαι.
2. εἰ τοῦτο πιστεύοι, εἴποι ἂν πᾶσιν. οὐδὲν γάρ τοι ἄξιον
τῆς πόλεως πεποίηκε.
3. τοὔνομα τοῦτο· ἐν μιᾷ τῶν ἡμερῶν· ἀνάστηθι, κύριε,
σῶσόν με, ὁ θεός μου.
4. τουτὶ δή ἐστι πάντων χαλεπώτατον πεῖσαί τινας ὑμῶν,
ὦ ἄνδρες Ἀθηναῖοι.
5. ἄμεινόν ἐστι σῶμά γ᾽ ἢ ψυχὴν νοσεῖν. ἅπαν θεοῦ μοι
δῶμ᾽, ἵν᾽ ἂν λάβῃ μ᾽ ὕπνος.
6. ἀλλ᾽, ὦ Σώκρατες, τὸ σὸν τί ἐστι πρᾶγμα; πόθεν αἱ
διαβολαί σοι αὗται γεγόνασιν;

(4: cf. Plato, *Apol.* 37e.5. 5b: Euripides, *Ion* 315. 6: Plato,
Apol. 20c.5.)

Lesson 8: Homework

1. φημὶ γάρ, ὦ ἄνδρες, οἳ ἐμὲ ἀπεκτόνατε, τιμωρίαν ὑμῖν ἥξειν εὐθύς.

2. ἀξιῶ καὶ δέομαι ὑμῶν εὐνοϊκῶς ἀκοῦσαί μου περὶ ὧν πέπονθα λέγοντος.

3. τυφλὸς τά τ' ὦτα τόν τε νοῦν τά τ' ὄμματ' εἶ.

4. κοὐδείς γέ μ' ἂν πείσειεν ἀνθρώπων τὸ μὴ οὐκ ἐλθεῖν ἐπ' ἐκεῖνον.

5. πότερον εἰς Ἅιδου κάτω; καὶ νὴ Δί' εἴ τί γ' ἔστιν ἔτι κατωτέρω.

6. Ἀχιλλῆος λάβε γούνατα καὶ κύσε χεῖρας δεινὰς ἀνδροφόνους.

(1: Plato, *Apol.* 39c.4. 2: cf. Demosthenes, *Conon* 2.
3: Sophocles, *Oed. tyr.* 371. 4: Aristophanes, *Frogs* 68.
5: Ibid., 69–70. 6: Homer, *Il.* 24.478–9.)

Further Practice 1

1. ἀγγελοῦσι, ἐπηρώτα, ἐφίλουν, ἐρεῖς, δηλοῦμεν, ἐπιζητεῖ.

2. τὸ συμφέρον τῇ πόλει, τοῦ παρόντος αἰῶνος, πολλὰ παθών.

3. ἐξῆλθον, συνεῖχον, ἵνα ἴδω, ἵνα εἰδῶ, ἵνα ᾖ, ἵνα ἀποδῶμεν.

4. γεγραμμένων, εἰδότα, πεποιηκώς, φυγών, μισούμενοι, ἐλθών.

5. θεάσασθαι, δοῦναι, ἀπιέναι, γενέσθαι, ποιῆσαι, πεποιῆσθαι.

6. μηκέτι ἐλθέ· περιβαλοῦ τὸ ἱμάτιον· εὐλογήσαι σε κύριος.

Further Practice 2

1. οὐδεὶς ἵππος ἐν τῷ ποταμῷ εἰ μὴ ἱπποπόταμος, ὕδατι ὄντι.

2. τίς ἄρα οὗτός ἐστιν; ὁ ποιμὴν ὁ καλὸς ἐκεῖνος ἢ ἕτερός τις;

3. τῶν παίδων εὖ ἐχόντων· κυνὸς εἰσιόντος· ἐκ πόλεών τινων.

4. αἱ νῆες οὖν εἰς τὸν λιμένα εἰσεδέχθησαν ὑπὸ τῶν πολιτῶν.

5. ὦ ἄνερ, ἔστι πᾶσι μία χεὶρ καὶ εἰς ποὺς ἐν τῇδε τῇ ζωῇ;

6. υἱὸς ἀγαπητός· ὁ μαθητὴς ὁ ἠγαπημένος· ἀδελφοὶ πιστοί.

Further Practice 3

1. ἡ δὲ τῆς βουλῆς γνώμη ἦν μιᾷ ψήφῳ ἅπαντας κρίνειν τοὺς ἄνδρας.

2. κατεψηφίσαντο τῶν στρατηγῶν ὀκτὼ ὄντων, ἀπέθανον δὲ οἱ παρόντες ἕξ.

3. ὕστερον δὲ στάσεώς τινος γενομένης, ἀπέδρασαν οὗτοι πρὶν κριθῆναι.

4. ἔθη ἃ οὐκ ἔξεστιν ἡμῖν παραδέχεσθαι Ῥωμαίοις οὖσιν.
5. ἰδόντες εἵλκυσαν αὐτοὺς εἰς τὴν ἀγορὰν ἐπὶ τοὺς ἄρχοντας.
6. πολλάς τε ἐπιθέντες αὐτοῖς πληγάς, ἔβαλον εἰς φυλακήν.

(1–3: cf. Xenophon, *Hell.* 1.7.34–5. 4–6: cf. NT, *Acts* 16:19, 21, 23.)

Further Practice 4

τὴν μὲν παρασκευήν, ὦ ἄνδρες, καὶ τὴν προθυμίαν τῶν ἐχθρῶν τῶν ἐμῶν, ὥστ᾽ ἐμὲ κακῶς ποιεῖν ἐκ παντὸς τρόπου, καὶ δικαίως καὶ ἀδίκως, ἐξ ἀρχῆς ἐπειδὴ τάχιστα ἀφικόμην εἰς τὴν πόλιν ταυτηνί, σχεδόν τι πάντες ἐπίστασθε, καὶ οὐδὲν δεῖ περὶ τούτων πολλοὺς λόγους ποιεῖσθαι. ἐγὼ δέ, ὦ ἄνδρες, δεήσομαι ὑμῶν δίκαια καὶ ὑμῖν τε ῥᾴδια χαρίζεσθαι καὶ ἐμοὶ ἄξια πολλοῦ τυχεῖν παρ᾽ ὑμῶν.

(Andocides, *Mysteries* 1.)

Further Practice 5

Σωκράτη φησὶν ἀδικεῖν τούς τε νέους διαφθείροντα καὶ θεοὺς οὓς ἡ πόλις νομίζει οὐ νομίζοντα, ἕτερα δὲ δαιμόνια καινά. τὸ μὲν δὴ ἔγκλημα τοιοῦτόν ἐστιν· τούτου δὲ τοῦ ἐγκλήματος ἓν ἕκαστον ἐξετάσωμεν. Φησὶ γὰρ δὴ τοὺς νέους ἀδικεῖν με διαφθείροντα. ἐγὼ δέ γε, ὦ ἄνδρες Ἀθηναῖοι, ἀδικεῖν φημι Μέλητον. . . . Καί μοι δεῦρο, ὦ Μέλητε, εἰπέ· ἄλλο τι ἢ περὶ πλείστου ποιῇ ὅπως ὡς βέλτιστοι οἱ νεώτεροι ἔσονται; Ἔγωγε. Ἴθι δή νυν εἰπὲ τούτοις, τίς αὐτοὺς βελτίους ποιεῖ;

(Plato, *Apology* 24b–d.)

Further Practice 6

τῇ δὲ μιᾷ τῶν σαββάτων ὄρθρου βαθέως ἐπὶ τὸ μνῆμα ἦλθον φέρουσαι ἃ ἡτοίμασαν ἀρώματα. εὗρον δὲ τὸν λίθον ἀποκεκυλισμένον ἀπὸ τοῦ μνημείου, εἰσελθοῦσαι δὲ οὐχ εὗρον τὸ σῶμα τοῦ κυρίου Ἰησοῦ. καὶ ἐγένετο ἐν τῷ ἀπορεῖσθαι αὐτὰς περὶ τούτου καὶ ἰδοὺ ἄνδρες δύο ἐπέστησαν αὐταῖς ἐν ἐσθῆτι ἀστραπτούσῃ. ἐμφόβων δὲ γενομένων αὐτῶν καὶ κλινουσῶν τὰ πρόσωπα εἰς τὴν γῆν εἶπαν πρὸς αὐτάς· τί ζητεῖτε τὸν ζῶντα μετὰ τῶν νεκρῶν; οὐκ ἔστιν ὧδε, ἀλλὰ ἠγέρθη.

(NT, *Luke* 24:1–6.)

Illustrations

1. Homer, *Iliad* 8.433, 435–47 + 434

Papyrus, I/II AD: PBerol. P. 6845.
Ägyptisches Museum und Papyrussammlung,
Staatliche Museen zu Berlin.

W. Schubart, *Papyri Graecae Berolinenses*, no. 19c.

ΛΥΤCΑΝΚΑΛΛΙΤ
ΝΠΡΟϹΕΝΙΩΠΙΛΠΛΛΙϢΛΝΟϢΝΠΛ
ΠϹΙΝΕΠΙΚΛΕΙϹΑΛΟΙϹΙΚΛΕΙΖΟΝ·
ΛΙΘΕΟΙϹΙΦΙΛΟΝΙΕΠΗΛΛΕΝΝΗΠΟΡ·
ΤΠΡΕΙΛΗΘΕΝΕΥΤΡΟΧΟΝΛΡΛΛΚΝΙΠΠΟΥϹ·
ΝΛΕΛΙΩΚΕΘΕΩΝΛΕΖΕΙΚΕΤΟΘΛΩΚΟΥϹ
ΠΠΟΥϹΛΛΕΝΛΥϹΕΝΚΛΥΤΟϹΕΝΝΟϹΙϝΑΙΟϹ·
ΛΞΙΩΛΟΙϹΙΤΙΘΕΙΚΛΤΛΛΕΙΤΛΠΕΤΛϹϹΛϹ·
ΤϹΕΙΟΗΕΠΙΘΡΟΝΟΝΕΥΡΥΟΠΛΖΕΥϹ
ΛΥΠΟΠΟϹϹΙΛΛΕΡΛΟΠΕΛΕΛΙΖΕΤϝΛΥΛΛΠΟϹ·
ΟΛΛΦΙϹΛΘΗΝΝΝΗΤΕΚΛΝΗΡΗ
ΛΧΕΠΛΛΙΝΤΙΡΟϹΕΦΩΝΕΟΝΟΥΛΕϝΕΟΝΤϹ·
ΙΩΗϹΙΝΕΝ··· ΕϹΙΦΩΝΗϹΕΝΤΕ·
ΟΤΕΤΙΗϹΘΟΝΛ···ΛΝΝΗΤΕΚΛΝΗΡΗ·

ΛΙΝΚΑΤΡΛΝϹΛΝϹ ΛΛΒΡΟϹΙΗϹΙΚΛΠΗϹΙΝ· ϰͦ

Notes

Accent markings first appear in poetic texts written on papyrus in the second century BC. Their invention is traditionally attributed to Aristophanes of Byzantium, head of the library of Alexandria early in that century. Over time they become increasingly common, until by the ninth century they are regularly written on every word. A codification of the system was compiled by Aelius Herodian in the second century AD. (See Probert, *New Short Guide*, 11–15.)

In this text, dating from I/II AD, they are used only sporadically, but in accordance with the traditional system. In the transcription, word-division has been introduced but the accents are those written on the papyrus. There are six uses of the acute and four of the circumflex; in addition, there are two of the diaeresis (ϋ), one breathing (in an early form: ⊦), and a mark like an apostrophe that divides two words and appears to indicate elision (πελεμιζετʼ ολυμπος). There is no consistent reason for the insertion of the accent marks, but they do help to identify words and word-breaks. So, e.g., λῦσεν in line 7 alerts the reader that it is a Homeric unaugmented aorist (= ἔλυσεν), which has a circumflex accent (cf. βῆν = ἔβην in lesson 8). Especially interesting is φωνησέν τε in line 13 (fully accented form φώνησέν τε): the person who inserted the accents made a point of marking the extra accent resulting from the enclitic following (cf. lesson 7).

The extra line (434) at the bottom was missed by the original scribe and has been added with the note ἄνω (= [insert] "above"). There was presumably a mark showing where to insert it, but we have lost that part of the papyrus.

[. . . με]ν λυσαν καλλιτριχ[ας . . .]

[. . . εκλιν]αν προς ενώπια παμφανόωντα·

[. . . χρυσε]οισιν επι κλεισμοισι κάθιζον·

[. . . αλλο]ισι θεοῖσι φιλον τετιημεναι ἤτορ·

[. . . πα]τηρ ειδηθεν εὔτροχον αρμα και ιππους·

[. . . ουλυμπο]νδε διωκε θεῶν δ εξέικετο θώκους

[. . . ι]ππους μεν λῦσεν κλυτος εννοσιγαιος·

[. . . α]μ βωμοῖσι τιθει κατα λειτα πετασσας·

[. . . χρ]υσειον επι θρονον ευρυοπα ζευς

[. . . τω]δ ὑπο ποσσι μεγας πελεμιζετ᾽ ολυμπος·

[. . . διο]ς αμφις αθηναιη τε και ηρη

[. . . ο]δε τι μιν προσεφωνεον ουδ ερεοντο·

[. . . εγν]ω ησιν ενι φ[ρ]εσι φωνησέν τε·

[. . . ουτ]ω τετιησθον αθηναιη τε και ηρη·

[. . . τους] μεν κατεδησαν ε[π] αμβροσιησι καπησιν· ανω

2. LXX Isaiah 13:3–8

Parchment codex, uncial script, VI AD:
Vat. gr. 2125 = OT MS Q (Codex Marchalianus),
folio 205r. © 2018 Biblioteca Apostolica Vaticana.

By permission of Biblioteca Apostolica
Vaticana, with all rights reserved.

B. M. Metzger, *Manuscripts of the Greek Bible*:
An Introduction to Palaeography
(Oxford: Oxford University Press, 1981), no. 21.

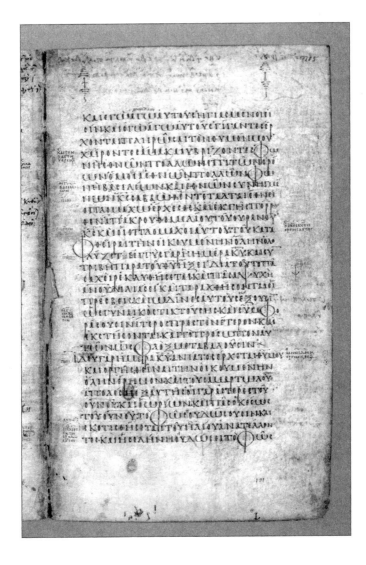

Notes

Accents and breathings are written consistently, but with some omissions (or perhaps they are just hard to read now in the MS). The placing on diphthongs is variable: they are mostly on the second vowel as usual, but sometimes on the first (e.g., line 1, κὰι) and sometimes in between (e.g., line 10, τοῦ). Breathings mostly have the archaic form seen in text 1. There is an apostrophe (line 10, ἀπ᾽ ἄκρου), and what appears to be a comma (line 10, after θεμελίου). Final -ν at the end of a line is twice indicated by a stroke jutting out from over the last letter (lines 13, 17). Abbreviated *nomina sacra* are indicated by a line above (e.g., line 11, κ(ύριο)ς).

The divine name (יהוה) is normally rendered κύριος in the LXX, but was written in Hebrew letters in some MSS. In this MS the Hebrew form is given in the margin, keyed to κ(ύριο)ς in the text. To represent the Hebrew form, Greek letters that roughly match the shape of the Hebrew letters (ΠΙΠΙ) are used (see lines 8, 11, 13). This MS is important for other marginal annotations indicating "Hexaplaric" readings in the LXX, that is, renderings of Aquila, Symmachus, and Theodotion. The readings are introduced by α′, σ′, θ′, or οἱ γ′ ("the three," i.e., all three of them), and keyed to the word in the text. For example, in line 7 the marginal note is οἱ γ′ βασιλειων (i.e., "the three have βασιλειῶν in their text"). It is keyed to βασιλέων by a wavy line. (On all this, see Metzger, *Manuscripts of the Greek Bible*, 35, 94.)

Transcription (lines 1–17)

κὰι ἐγὼ ἄγω αὐτούς· ἡγιασμένοι εἰσίν καὶ ἐγὼ ἄγω αὐτούς· γίγαντες ἔρχονται πληρῶσαι τὸν θυμόν μου·
χαίροντες ἅμα καὶ ὑβρίζοντες· φω-
νὴ ἐθνῶν πολλῶν ἐπι τῶν ὀρέ-
ων· ὁμοία ἐθνῶν πολλῶν φω-
νὴ βασιλέων. κὰι ἐθνῶν συνηγμέ-
νων· κ(υριο)ς σαβαὼθ ἐντέταλται ἔθνει
ὁπλομάχω· ἔρχεσθε καὶ ἐκ γῆς πόρρω-
θεν· ἀπ' ἄκρου θεμελίου, τοῦ οὐρανοῦ·
κ(ύριο)ς καὶ οἱ ὁπλομάχοι αὐτοῦ. τοῦ κατα-
φθεῖραι τὴν οἰκουμένην ὅλην· ὀλο-
λύζετε ἐγγὺς γὰρ ἡ ἡμέρα κ(υριο)υ. κὰι συν-
τριβὴ παρα τοῦ θ(εο)υ ἥξει· διὰ τοῦτο πᾶσα χεὶρ ἐκλυθήσεται· κὰι πᾶσα ψυχὴ
αν(θρωπ)ου δειλιάσει· καὶ ταραχθήσονται οἱ
πρέσβεις κὰι ὠδῖνες αὐτοὺς ἕξουσιν

3. NT Romans 14:22–23 + 16:25–27

Parchment codex, minuscule script, XIV AD: Univ.
Michigan Ms. 34 = CSNTM GA 223 0144a.

By permission of the Special Collections Library,
University of Michigan, and The Center for the Study
of New Testament Manuscripts (www.csntm.org).

B. M. Metzger, *Manuscripts of the Greek Bible*, no. 43.

Μακάριος ὁ μὴ κρίνων ἑαυτὸν
ἐν ᾧ δοκιμάζει· ὁ δὲ διακρι-
νόμενος, ἐὰν φάγῃ κατακέ-
κριται, ὅτι οὐκ ἐκ πίστεως·
πᾶν δὲ ὃ οὐκ ἐκ πίστεως, ἁ-
μαρτία ἐστίν· Τῷ δὲ δυναμένῳ ὑμᾶς στηρίξαι κατὰ τὸ εὐαγγέ-
λιόν μου καὶ τὸ κήρυγμα Ἰυ Χυ
κατὰ ἀποκάλυψιν μυστηρί-
ου χρόνοις αἰωνίοις σεσιγημένου
φανερωθέντος δὲ νῦν· διά τε
γραφῶν προφητικῶν κατ'
ἐπιταγὴν τοῦ αἰωνίου θυ
εἰς ὑπακοὴν πίστεως· εἰς
πάντα τὰ ἔθνη γνωρισθέν-
τος μόνῳ σοφῷ θω διὰ Ἰυ Χυ· ᾧ
ἡ δόξα εἰς τοὺς αἰῶνας ἀμήν·
Ὀφείλομεν δὲ ἡμεῖς οἱ δυνατοὶ
τὰ ἀσθενήματα τῶν ἀδυνά-
των βαστάζειν· Καὶ μὴ ἑαυτοῖς
ἀρέσκειν· ἕκαστος ἡμῶν τῷ πλη-
σίον ἀρεσκέτω εἰς τὸ ἀγαθὸν

κη̅ | τε̅ ·πρ̅ τ̅ ἡμῶν τη̅ς τοῦ χ̅υ̅ ἀπαθ̅ | κακίας·

Notes

This beautiful minuscule hand employs many ligatures, following the conventions of the time. The same letters may take on different shapes, either to suit the letters that accompany them or for reasons of space: see, e.g., the different shapes of εἰς in the last four lines. Accents and breathings are carefully marked, even on abbreviated words, like ἰ(ησο)ῦ χ(ριστο)ῦ (line 8): there is a line over each word to indicate abbreviation *and* a circumflex above that. The diaeresis is written frequently over iota (ϊ) and sometimes over upsilon (ϋ), a practice found in many MSS. This diaeresis may on occasion serve its original purpose of indicating that ι or υ, which might combine with the preceding vowel to form one sound, is to be separated (see examples in lesson 8), but usually it is "to help the reader pick out ι or υ" (Metzger, *Manuscripts of the Greek Bible*, 13).

The location of Rom. 16:25–27, the "doxology" (τῷ δὲ δυναμένῳ . . . ἀμήν), varies in the MSS. This MS, along with most representatives of the Byzantine text, incorporates it here after 14:23, while others place it at the end of the Epistle.

This codex, containing Acts and the Epistles, was also used for readings in church services. It has marginal markings indicating the start and end of each reading and when it is to be read. Our passage is the last part of a reading that begins on the previous page (Rom. 14:19 ἄρα οὖν . . .). In the right margin next to ἀμήν, the marginal note first indicates the end of that reading: τέ(λος) σα(ββάτῳ) = "end of [reading] on Saturday"; then the rest relates to the next reading: ἀνά(γνωσμα) ο, κυ(ριακῇ) ζ = "reading 70, on Sunday 7." In the left margin ἀρχ(ή) is written to indicate the beginning of the reading (Rom. 15:1 ὀφείλομεν . . .).

Transcription (lines 1–17)

Μακάριος ὁ μὴ κρίνων ἑαυτὸν

ἐν ᾧ δοκϊμάζει· ὁ δὲ δϊακρϊ

νόμενος, ἐὰν φάγη κατακέ

κρϊται. ὅτϊ οὐκ ἐκ πῖστεως·

πᾶν δὲ ὃ οὐκ ἐκ πίστεως, ἁ

μαρτία ἐστϊ· τῷ δὲ δυναμένω

ὑμᾶς στηρῖξαι κατὰ τὸ εὐαγγέ

λϊόν μου καὶ τὸ κήρυγμα ἱ(ησο)ῦ χ(ριστο)ῦ.

κατὰ ἀποκάλυψιν μϋστηρίου

χρόνοις αἰωνῖοις σεσϊγημένου.

Φανερωθέντος δὲ νῦν· δϊά τε

γραφῶν προφητϊκῶν κατ᾽

ἐπιταγὴν τοῦ αἰωνίου θ(εο)ῦ

εἰς ὑπακοὴν πίστεως· εἰς

πάντα τὰ ἔθνη γνωρϊσθέντο[ς]·

μόνω σοφῷ θ(ε)ῷ δϊὰ ἱ(ησο)ῦ χ(ριστο)ῦ· ᾧ

ἡ δόξα εἰς τοὺς αἰῶνας ἀμήν:

4. Demosthenes, *On the Crown* §§119–20

Printed book: Αἰσχίνου ὁ κατὰ Κτησιφῶντος καὶ Δημοσθένους ὁ
περὶ στεφάνου λόγος: cum delectu annotationum, praecipue
E Tayloro, Marklando, Reiskio. Editio secunda (Oxonii: e
typographeo Clarendoniano, 1807), 67. Author's copy.

ΠΕΡΙ ΣΤΕΦΑΝΟΥ. 67

τῶ Ἀθηναίων, καὶ ϛεφανῶσαι χρυσῷ ϛεφάνῳ, καὶ ἀνα-
γορεῦσαι τὸν ϛέφανον ἐν τῷ θεάτρῳ, Διονυσίοις, Τραγῳ-
δοῖς καινοῖς· τῆς δὲ ἀναγορεύσεως ἐπιμεληθῆναι τὸν
Ἀγωνοθέτην.

λς΄. Οὐκοῦν, ἃ μὲν ἐπέδαιξα, ταῦτ᾽ ἐϛὶν, ὧν οὐδὲν
σὺ γέγραψαι· ἃ δὲ φησιν ἡ βουλὴ δεῖν ἀντὶ τούτων γενέσθαι μοι, ταῦτ᾽ ἐϛ᾽ ἃ διώκεις. Τὸ λαβεῖν οὖν τὰ δι-
δόμενα ὁμολογῶν ἔννομον ἔι, τὸ χάριν τύτων ἀποδοῦναι
ἀθανόμων γράφει; Ὁ δὲ παμπόνηρος ἄνθρωπος, καὶ
θεοῖς ἐχθρὸς κ̀ βάσκανος ὄντως, ποῖός τις ἂν εἴη πρὸς
θεῶν, οὐχ ὁ τοιοῦτος; Καὶ μὴν περὶ τῷ γ᾽ ἐν τῷ
θεάτρῳ κηρύττεσθαι, τὸ μὲ μυριάκις μυρίας κεκηρύχθαι,
ἀθαλείπω, καὶ τὸ πολλάκις αὐτὸς ἐϛεφανῶσθαι πρό-
τερον· ἀλλὰ πρὸς θεῶν, οὕτω σκαιὸς εἶ, καὶ ἀναίσθη-
τος, Αἰσχίνη, ὥϛ᾽ οὐ δύνασαι λογίσασθαι, ὅτι τῷ μὲν
ϛεφανουμένῳ τὸν αὐτὸν ἔχει ζῆλον ὁ ϛέφανος, ὅπου ἂν
ἀναρρηθῇ· τῷ δὲ τῶν ϛεφανέντων ἕνεκα συμφέροντος ἐν
τῷ θεάτρῳ γίγνεται τὸ κήρυγμα; Οἱ γὰρ ἀκούσαντες
ἅπαντες εἰς τὸ ποιεῖν εὖ τὴν πόλιν προτρέπονται, καὶ
τὺς ἀποδιδόντας τὴν χάριν μᾶλλον ἐπαινοῦσι τῷ ϛεφα-
νομένῳ· διόπερ τ νόμον τῦτον ἡ πόλις γέγραφε. Λέγε
δ᾽ αὐτόν μοι τὸν νόμον λαβών.

NOMOΣ.

ΟΣΟΥΣ ϛεφανοῦσί τινες τῶν δήμων, τὰς ἀναγο-
ρεύσεὶς τῶν ϛεφάνων ποιεῖσθαι ἐν αὐτοῖς ἑκάϛους τοῖς
ἰδίοις δήμοις, ἐὰν μή τινας ὁ δῆμος ὁ τῶν Ἀθηναίων, ἢ

T 2

Notes

The first printed books of the fifteenth century replicated the handwriting of the time, which used many ligatures and variant forms of letters. The early printers prided themselves on the rich abundance of their fonts and their ability to reproduce something like a handwritten manuscript. The use of such fonts was not universal, but it did continue for centuries, even down to the early nineteenth century, as in this example.

As can be seen, accents (and breathings) are carefully included, even in the more extreme ligatures, such as μὲν in line 8 and εἶναι in line 4. In some cases the accent is incorporated into the ligature, as in τῷ at the end of line 7. The circumflex in this font takes a "tilde" form, which derives from handwriting of the fifteenth century; the other, rounded shape is found at the same time. In this text we see the earlier practice of retaining a grave accent before a comma (as in ἐστὶν, in line 1), where today's convention is to write an acute before any mark of punctuation (see lesson 1).

Transcription (lines 5–18)

Οὐκοῦν, ἃ μὲν ἐπέδωκα, ταῦτ᾽ ἐστὶν, ὧν οὐδὲν
σὺ γέγραψαι· ἃ δέ φησιν ἡ βουλὴ δεῖν ἀντὶ τούτων γενέσθαι μοι, ταῦτ᾽ ἔσθ᾽ ἃ διώκεις. Τὸ λαβεῖν οὖν τὰ δι-
δόμενα ὁμολογῶν ἔννομον εἶναι, τὸ χάριν τούτων
    ἀποδοῦναι
παρανόμων γράφῃ; Ὁ δὲ παμπόνηρος ἄνθρωπος, καὶ
θεοῖς ἐχθρὸς καὶ βάσκανος ὄντως, ποῖός τις ἂν εἴη πρὸς
θεῶν; οὐχ ὁ τοιοῦτος; Καὶ μὴν περὶ τοῦ γ᾽ ἐν τῷ
θεάτρῳ κηρύττεσθαι, τὸ μὲν μυριάκις μυρίους
    κεκηρύχθαι,
παραλείπω, καὶ τὸ πολλάκις αὐτὸς ἐστεφανῶσθαι πρό-
τερον· ἀλλὰ πρὸς θεῶν, οὕτω σκαιὸς εἶ, καὶ ἀναίσθη-
τος, Αἰσχίνη, ὥστ᾽ οὐ δύνασθαι λογίσασθαι, ὅτι τῷ μὲν
στεφανουμένῳ τὸν αὐτὸν ἔχει ζῆλον ὁ στέφανος, ὅπου ἂν
ἀναρρηθῇ· τοῦ δὲ τῶν στεφανούντων ἕνεκα συμφέροντος ἐν
τῷ θεάτρῳ γίγνεται τὸ κήρυγμα;

Greek Word Index

The index of words provides a means of checking the accents of words encountered in the exercises. Where useful, it also indicates the lesson in which a word or form was introduced or explained. It is not exhaustive, however, and some use of a grammar or lexicon will be needed (in fact is encouraged), especially in completing the homework exercises. In the case of the Further Practice exercises, no help is given. References are to *lesson numbers*.

ἀγαγεῖν
ἀγαθός
ἀγγεῖλαι, 2
ἅγιος
ἀγορά
ἀγών
ἄδελφε, 8
ἀδελφός
ἀδικία, 3
ἄδικος
Ἀθήναζε
Ἀθηναῖος
Ἅιδης, 8
ἀΐδιος, 8

αἰσχύνη
αἴτιος
ἀκούσας, 5
ἀκούων, 5
ἀλήθεια
ἀληθῆ, 6
ἀληθής
ἀληθοῦς, 6
ἀλλά
ἀλλήλων
ἄλλος
ἄν
ἀνά
ἀναβάς, 5

ἀναστάς, 5
ἀνήρ, 3
ἄνθρωπος
ἄνθρωπος, 8
ἄνοια
ἀντιλαβοῦ, 2
ἄνω
ἀξία, 3
ἄξιος
ἅπας
ἄπειμι
ἀπεῖναι, 2
ἄπειπε
ἀπεῖπον, 2

εἰδώς, 5

εἰμι

εἰμί, 8

εἰμι, 7

εἶναι, 2

εἰπέ, 2

εἰπέμεν, 8

εἰπέτε, 2

εἶπον

εἷς, 4

εἰς

εἰσῆλθον, 2

εἰσι, 7

εἴτε

εἶχον

ἐκ

ἔκβολος, 8

ἐκεῖ

ἐκεῖνος, 4

ἐκθοῦ, 2

ἐκκλησία

ἔκπλους, 6

ἐλθέ, 2

ἐλθεῖν, 2

ἐλθέτε, 2

ἔλιπον

ἐλπίς

ἐμέ, 4, 7

ἔμμεναι, 8

ἐμοί, 4, 7

ἐμοῦ, 4, 7

ἕν, 4

ἐν

ἐναντίος

ἔνδοξος, 8

ἐνθάδε

ἔνι, 8

ἐντολή

ἐξέσται

ἔξεστι

ἔξω

ἐπεί

ἐπειδή

ἐπί

ἔπι, 8

ἔρημος

ἔρχομαι

ἐρῶ, 6

ἐσμεν, 7

ἐστε, 7

ἔστι, 8

ἐστι, 7

ἑστῶτες, 6

ἔσω

ἕτερος

ἔτι

ἔτος

εὖ

εὔνοια

εὐνοϊκῶς, 8

εὔνους, 6

εὑρέ, 2

ἔφη

ἔχω

ἑώρα, 6

ἑώρων, 6

ἕως

ἤ

ἡγεμών, 3

ἡδεῖα, 5

ἥδιον, 8

ἡδίων, 8

ἡδύς

ἦλθον

ἡμεῖς, 4

ἡμέρα

ἠώς, 8

θάλασσα

θάλαττα

θεά

θεός

θυγάτηρ

ἰατρός

ἰδέ, 2

ἴδε, 2

ἰδεῖν

ἴδετε, 2

ἱερός

ἵνα

ἰών, 5

ὁδός

οἱ, 8

οἴκαδε

οἰκία

ὀλίγος

ὄνομα

ὅπως

ὅς, ἥ, ὅ

ὅστις, 8

ὅτε

ὅτι

οὐ, 8

οὔ, οὐκ, οὐχ

οὔ, 8

οὐδέ

οὐδείς, 4

οὐκέτι

οὔκουν, 8

οὐκοῦν, 8

οὖν

οὐσῶν, 5

οὔτε

οὗτος, 4

οὑτοσί, 8

οὐχί

ὀφθαλμός

παιδεῦσαι, 2

παιδίον

παίδων, 8

παῖς

πάϊς, 8

πάλιν

πάντων, 3, 8

παρά

πάρα, 8

παράλαβε

παράσχου, 2

παρεῖδον, 2

παρθένος

πᾶς, 3

πασῶν, 5

πατήρ, 3

περ, 7

περί

πέρι, 8

περίβολος, 8

περίθες, 2

περίπλους, 6

πληγή

πλήρης

πλοῖον

πλοῦς, 6

πνεῦμα

πόθεν, 7

ποθεν, 7

ποῖ, 7

ποι, 7

πολέμοιο, 8

πόλεμος

πόλεως, 8

πόλις, 3

πολιτεία

πολίτεω, 8

πολίτης

πολύς, 4

ποταμός

πότε, 7

ποτε, 7

ποῦ, 7

που, 7

πούς

πρᾶγμα

πρᾶξαι, 2

πραῢς, 8

πρέσβεις

πρίν

πρό

πρόβατον

πρόθυμος

πρός

πρόσχωμεν, 8

προφήτης

πρωΐ, 8

πρῶτος

πῶς, 7

πως, 7

ῥῆμα

σάρξ

σαφής

σέ, 4, 7

Subject Index

R eferences are to *lesson numbers*.